Emma Raymond Pitman

Missionary Heroines in eastern Lands

Woman's Work in Mission Fields

Emma Raymond Pitman

Missionary Heroines in eastern Lands
Woman's Work in Mission Fields

ISBN/EAN: 9783743331693

Manufactured in Europe, USA, Canada, Australia, Japa

Cover: Foto ©ninafisch / pixelio.de

Manufactured and distributed by brebook publishing software (www.brebook.com)

Emma Raymond Pitman

Missionary Heroines in eastern Lands

PREFACE.

THE annals of Christian Missions furnish copious records of womanly heroism. From the days of Ann H. Judson, in the early part of this century, until now, the succession has not failed. Alike in the frozen regions of Greenland and under the tropical heats of India delicate women have been found labouring side by side with their husbands among their untaught, heathen sisters. The records of mission toil prove that they have not laboured in vain, nor spent their strength for nought. As the fruits of their self-denial, that "Great Day for which all other days were made" will see multitudes who shall be their reward and crown of rejoicing. As we think of reward, we turn to the days of Christ upon earth, when He told His disciples that, as they had followed Him through contumely, and hatred, and kingly persecution, so, "great should be their reward in heaven." This may safely be said of these missionary toilers. They followed their Master in His self-denial and labour for others, and they will share in the honours of His kingdom.

Mrs. Mackay Ruthquist's life among the Hindoo peoples, furnishes some new light on mission work in that land; Mrs. Bowen Thompson's work in Syria opens up a comparatively new field of mission life; Miss McGeorge's deals with the medical aspect of missions in the East, showing how necessary and beneficial it is that the missionary should imitate his Master in being a healer and a teacher; while Miss Whately's life commends itself as a record of self-sacrifice among the peasants of the Nile. In all these instances it will be found that to women, animated with the true Spirit, open doors were very numerous. It is needless to attempt to tabulate results in either of these cases. They worked for eternity, sowing the sure seed of the kingdom which infallibly bears abundant harvest.

We look upon it as a great honour conferred upon stay-at-home Christians to be permitted to sustain the hands of these far-away workers; to be permitted to count one such worker upon a family roll is a patent of heaven's nobility. Those who have given friends to this high and holy enterprise may rest assured that the gift is honoured by the Master, and will redound in blessings on those whom they have left behind.

In conclusion, it remains for me to thank those who have rendered me aid in the compilation of this little volume of biographies. More particularly do I extend my thanks to E. G. McGeorge, Esq., J.P., of Belfast, who kindly furnished me with MS. assistance relating to his sister's life. Her memory must be to his family, as well as to the Irish Presbyterian Church, a very sweet savour of cheerful self-surrender, and a suddenly yielded life.

E. R. P

CONTENTS.

		PAGE
I. MRS. ALEXINA MACKAY RUTHQUIST,		8
1. Early Life,		9
2. Access to Heathen Homes,		13
3. More Zenana Work,		18
4. Evangelistic Village Work,		24
5. Sowing beside all Waters,		29
II. MRS. BOWEN THOMPSON,		40
1. Beginnings,		41
2. School Work,		51
3. Encouragements,		59
4. Closing Days in Syria,		69
III. DR. MARY McGEORGE,		76
1. Early Days—Consecration and Training,		77
2. The New Sphere of Work,		82
3. Heathen Manners and Customs,		93
4. Life in Ahmedabad,		99
5. Medical Work,		107
6. Work among the Villages,		116
7. Home,		121
IV. MISS MARY LOUISA WHATELY,		128
1. The Preparation,		129
2. Beginning Work,		139
3. Sowing beside all Waters,		148

MRS. ALEXINA MACKAY RUTHQUIST.

(*From Photo by H Gordon, Aberdeen.*)

… MISSIONARY HEROINES IN EASTERN LANDS.

Mrs. Alexina Mackay Ruthquist,

A SINGER OF GOOD NEWS AMONG HINDOO PEOPLES.

CHAPTER I.

EARLY LIFE.

MRS. ALEXINA RUTHQUIST was the daughter of the Rev. M. Mackay, the Free Church minister of Fordyce, a little village on the Banffshire coast of Scotland; she was born there on the 8th of September, 1848. We are told that Alexina "was a merry little girl, full of rhyme and repartee," and when very young, was wont, out of pure kindliness of heart, to visit blind, deaf, and afflicted ones in the hamlet, and to do her childish best to enliven and cheer their loneliness. It is likely that Alexina had heard much of missions in her childhood, for her maternal grandfather, the Rev. John Robertson, was a staunch advocate of them, even in the early part of this century; and it is by no means an uninteresting fact that no fewer than four of Mr. Robertson's granddaughters have devoted their lives to work in foreign mission-fields.

It would seem that Alexina's enthusiasm for missions, and the design of devoting her life to them, grew and matured, unknown to her friends, till the point of decision was reached while she was away at school in the city of Edinburgh. We are told that she immediately wrote home, and acquainted her parents with her resolution; but that while the father saw, like Eli of old, "that the Lord had called the child," the mother could not speak for tears. She had, both by example and precept, trained up her children to look forward to the Lord's service as the noblest service, but "little had she dreamed—as she and her husband had patiently, and with much wrestling with God in prayer, not only sought to make their children choose the better part, but had also, with quite exceptional care, endeavoured to fashion and mould their lives after the Divine pattern—that in the dim horizon of the future there was awaiting Alexina a lone bungalow, on the outskirts of a dirty city, teeming with idolaters, under a tropical sun, and in a land of pestilence, storm, and cyclone." The blessing Mrs. Mackay had sought so eagerly and believingly was not at first received joyfully. Her heart ached at the thought of parting with Alexina, even to engage in the much-loved missionary work.

But a waiting-time of some years came to the school-girl, and in 1876 Alexina was occupying the post of governess in the family of Mr. Cowan, banker, at Alva, in Stirlingshire. Early in that year the Committee of the Free Church of Scotland Ladies' Society for Female Education in India and South

Africa needed a lady missionary to go to the East, and made inquiries among various ministerial friends. One friend replied: "I know the family of a Free Church minister, where there are several girls—all pious—for they have the inestimable blessing of a mother who spends much of her time in secret prayer. If you can secure one of them you will do well."

A communication was immediately sent to Mr. Mackay, and he forwarded the letter to his daughter. We may imagine with what startled, grateful surprise Miss Mackay would regard this letter. The call had evidently come at last! She said of it herself, writing back:—"Many thoughts have come upon me since I received your kind letter, charged with such weighty contents. I will tell you simply how I feel in regard to this most important subject, and may God over-rule the whole matter for His own glory and our good. Well, when I read your letter, a burst of grateful surprise took possession of me, since it seemed to me that here, at last, I had got the call to go forth to the work I had many a time longed to be permitted to be engaged in; and at once I submitted the matter to God's hands, that He might dispose of it as He thought fit. With Him, then, I desire that it may rest. I feel that it would be a great privilege to be permitted to enter the lists with those favoured few who have been called to bear the 'lamp of life' into the dark corners of the earth; and if, in the providence of God, I am called to that honour, I desire to respond, 'Here I am!' and to venture forward on the unknown, untried path."

Finally, Mrs. Mackay fully recognised the hand of God in the matter, and herself conveyed the answer written by Alexina to the sitting Committee of the Aberdeen Auxiliary Branch of the Society. She felt that she could no longer refuse to recognise God's answer to the prayers which for years she had been putting up in her daughter's behalf.

The next step was taken when Alexina went to Edinburgh and met the general Committee of the Society, who engaged her on a three years' term, as was their custom, for service in India, though at the time it was not certainly known whether Calcutta or Nagpoor was to be her home. She was required at one of these centres to assist among the Zenanas, and her bright, sunny disposition fitted her exactly for the work, for it is not exaggeration to say that Zenana dwellers have the most cheerless lives under heaven. Witness, in confirmation, the despairing petitions of a Hindoo lady, as recorded by an American lady: "O Lord, hear my prayer! For ages dark ignorance has brooded over our minds and spirits; like a cloud of dust it rises and wraps us round; and we are like prisoners in an old and mouldy house, choked and buried in the dust of custom, and we have no strength to get out. Bruised and beaten, we are like the dry husks of the sugar-cane when the sweet juice has been extracted. Criminals confined in jails are happier than we are, for they know something of Thy world. They were not born in prison; but we have not, for one day, no, not even in our dreams, seen Thy world; we cannot know Thee, its maker. We have been born in this jail; we have died here, and are dying. O God of mercies, our prayer to Thee is this, that the curse may be removed from the women of India."

Miss Mackay was finally appointed to Zenana work at Nagpoor, where the Rev. J. G. Cooper and Mrs. Cooper were already carrying on a mission successfully. Mrs. Cooper found Miss Mackay to be so valuable a helper, that she wrote gratefully at the end of a year to the Missionary Committee: "At the close of a year, I cannot help writing to thank you for the valuable help you gave us when you sent dear Miss Mackay, and the wisdom you showed in electing her. We truly needed help; and Miss Mackay has proved herself equal to the work, and been able to carry it on with vigour, so that we have every cause to thank God for so guiding you, and inclining your hearts to help us."

CHAPTER II.

ACCESS TO HEATHEN HOMES.

IT is difficult for any Englishwoman to enter into the full degradation and discomfort of a Hindoo woman's life, especially if she belong to the richer class. The higher-class women are strictly shut up inside the high walls and dark rooms of their Zenanas. Their houses are not like English homes, comfortable or pretty, but the rudest, dirtiest, and most uncomfortable that can be imagined. According to Mrs. Ruthquist's biographer, "Hindoo homes are very dirty and dusty. Even the ladies' apartments have little appearance of culture, or even of comfort, and are most sparely furnished. Hideous pictures of gods and goddesses (and there are three hundred and thirty millions of these), adorn the walls, but there are seldom flowers or ferns, or books, or musical instruments, or anything to suggest the presence of the gentler sex. Dogs swarm in the rooms, and hens, chickens, and even crows are allowed to remain unmolested, and perch on the bedsteads, or anywhere they choose; as part of the Hindoo worship is that birds and beasts must be fed. The homes of the Mohammedans are, of course, equally unattractive, but with them 'no dogs are admitted.'"

Among other reminiscences of idolatry, we are told that the Queen Dowager of the Rajah of Nagpoor, when dying, was directed to lay hold of the tail of one of the sacred cows, which was led into her presence for the purpose by a Brahmin, under the belief that it would drag her, at the moment of death, into heaven. It was to such ignorant women, and to such homes as these that Miss Mackay was deputed to minister, as Zenana teacher and worker. But before doing much, she had to acquire the Marathi language, and we are told that she displayed such unusual proficiency in the acquirement of it, that "within six months she was able to sing native hymns, and to read the Scriptures to the inmates of the Zenanas to which she gained access."

Of course, the circumstances of the homes to which she gained access were very varied. Our readers will understand this for themselves, if we here transcribe part of the first year's Report sent to the Committee at home. It is so interesting that we would fain give it all, but the exigencies of space forbid.

"Perhaps the most interesting mode of giving in my Report of my first year's experiences of Zenana visiting in Nagpoor will be by asking my friends to accompany me in imagination on my various rounds in the city, taking up each day's work as it comes in succession.

"To begin with Monday. A pleasant drive along a country road skirted with trees, and lying at the city end of it, along an extensive, picturesque-looking tank, leads us into the city; and after threading our way through a couple of streets, a lane, and an alley, we reach our first house. On entering the narrow old wooden door leading into the yard, the first thing that meets the eye is a mass of weedy luxuriance, occupying a spot in the yard which might be turned

"GRINDING THE MORNING'S SUPPLIES."

to better account, while in another corner stands a painted clay model of a sacred bull, in close proximity to which two women are busy grinding the morning's supplies by turning in conjunction a round flat stone with a handle in the middle, upon a similarly-shaped one beneath. 'Salaam,' we say, and pass on round the house to the outside room we occupy while teaching. Something in the shape of a carpet has been thrown down on the floor, and an old chair, in preparation for the arrival of 'Missé Baba,' as I am termed; and after a few minutes' waiting we are joined by Sukyabai and her mother, Lodubai, both nice-looking women, and both pupils, the mother having first urged on her daughter to acquire the art of reading, and requesting latterly to be taught herself. Four little girls from the neighbouring houses attend here as well, and listeners often drop in. We begin by singing a hymn, and explaining the meaning of it; the effect of this opening exercise is wonderful upon those who are present for the first time. Times are surely changed when we can fearlessly open fire upon a group of heathen men, women, and children, and attempt to storm their prejudices by singing out such words as these,—'Why do you toil in vain? Bathing, and going on pilgrimage, and all your many pilgrimages, and all your many ceremonies will profit you nothing,' the only result being an interchange of looks of pleased surprise, with perhaps an attempt at argument afterwards, on the part of some zealous believer in the 'Shasters.' After we have sung, I am in the habit of reading aloud, either a passage from the New Testament, or a portion from some nice tract or adaptation of Scripture; but, for the most part, I have as yet to leave the explanatory part to Amundai, the native Bible-woman who accompanies me, or to employ a young friend from the Orphanage to convey my thoughts to the listeners. It is not easy for one living among English people to acquire a foreign language, conversationally; still, I do not scruple to make attempts to converse with my native friends, and I may report, for the comfort of my friends, that I am well understood.

"On Tuesday we visit another and very distant quarter of the city, where eight houses are open to us. I cannot visit all these during one morning, so I mean to divide the labour, and go once a-week to each four.

IN THE ZENANA.

In this way I shall be able to spend more time in the various houses, and to get more satisfactory work done, though the visits must be less frequent. In the first of these houses, separated in some cases by considerable distances, live a most respectable Brahmin family —father, mother, widowed daughter, and some others, related to each other, I don't quite know how. There is another widow with such a sweet-looking little boy. Beside these, several friends came in from time to time; amongst others, a very respectable-looking man, a son of the old Brahmin at the head of the house, who keeps a school next door, and also some of his boy-pupils. . . . A little way off lives a Brahmin widow, such a happy-looking old woman, in spite of her shorn head. In her house we have four pupils, one of them her little pet, a grandchild, in whose lesson on the alphabet she eagerly joined one day by way of encouraging the child, who was rather shy. Near this house is another, where a number of showy-looking women assemble, some of whom are avoided by their neighbours on account of the low platform of morality they occupy. . . . But it would be tedious to enumerate all the houses visited. I have access at present to sixteen houses, and I find that I have twenty-nine pupils."

CHAPTER III.

MORE ZENANA WORK.

IN the last chapter we find that sixteen houses and twenty-nine pupils comprised the number within the circle of Miss Mackay's influence and teaching. But as time went on, she was received with cordiality into other homes — notably, many other Brahmin ones; and was permitted to teach a good number of the wives and daughters of Brahmins. Occasionally, she had to combat opposition on the

A BRAHMIN GIRL.

part of the husbands to their wives receiving instruction, more especially religious instruction in the Gospel of Christ, so that she had to overcome prejudices and opposition by degrees. Her bright winning manner, however, and her talent for hymn-singing stood her in good stead. In the end, she generally gained her way, as the following instance will show :—

The husband of a woman whom she was visiting, put the following note into her hand: "My dear madam,—I hope you will excuse me to express my opinion in regards teaching of our women. I am strictly of opinion that no books or sermons adverse to the religion in which the learner is brought up, should be taught or preached, unless, and not until they have acquired sufficient strength of mind not to be led away by the superficial light. This strength, I perceive, cannot be obtained unless they advance in their study. For the present, I think you will kindly stick to rudimentary teachings and needlework, and such other fine things which are essential to a family woman."

Miss Mackay discontinued her visits, but she had an interview with the husband, at his wife's request, and so gained his respect and confidence that he accepted portions of the Bible, promising to study them carefully. He had been educated in the Government school of the city, and could read well. Accordingly Miss Mackay promised him a complete copy of the Bible, as soon as he had read the two Gospel portions. Finally, before many days had passed, a message was sent to Miss Mackay, requesting her to resume her visits to the house, as the wife missed her teaching so much.

In the Hindoo religious teaching there is no sound

of sin or sinfulness. Hindoos never ask their gods to take away their sins. They offer their idols presents, in sacrifices, to *please* them, but never in the sense of *making atonement* for sin. Descriptions of heaven as a holy place seem to be above their comprehension; but when, to a group of poor downtrodden women, heaven is pictured as a place where there is no death, neither pain nor tears, they can receive and understand it.

A gentleman of the Indian Civil Service, in his address at the Centenary Conference on Missions, some time since, speaking of the value of hymn-singing among the natives, on the part of mission-workers, observes: "Let me remind you how important a part hymnology must play—how important it is to take the native lute, and to train up men who go into the villages, with their lutes, to sing the Gospel. We want the Gospel sung in such a way that every native, high or low, shall listen to it. We want to get down to the masses, to their every-day life, and, if we can, to saturate that with the blessed principles of the Gospel of Christ." Miss Mackay acted out this teaching in her every-day visits among the people. Two incidents proved to her how welcome these singings were. "Once I was promised a piece (a copper coin less than a halfpenny in value), if I would sing a hymn to a crowd of people gathered in and around the verandah of a house." Again—"One blind old man, sitting beside me had a long story to tell me, in the course of which he was checked by his neighbour, who wished to hear the end of my story about why I had left my native land. The blind man said that he had heard me sing somewhere else, and had been longing to hear me again."

In this connection, it is almost fairer and certainly more interesting to give her own account of her domiciliary visits. We therefore transcribe one account in full.

"Some time ago you may remember that we made bold to go up to a native school, which was held in a large verandah facing the street, in hope of securing some openings through the influence of the master, or at best, of being allowed to sing a hymn to the assembled boys. Well, we were allowed to sing, but although we paid a second visit soon after, to inquire as to the result of our intimation made to the children of our readiness to visit their homes, we had no encouragement given us, as no one wished to learn.

"On a subsequent day, however, we learnt that a woman living in an upper story of the building, was very anxious to see us. This was good news, and we soon presented ourselves in the large verandah, from whence the school had adjourned somewhere else, to inquire after her. We got rather a rough reception, however, from an old Brahmin, who had lain down to sleep there. He told us that 'we had no concern with them, indeed,' so that we had to withdraw. On hearing again that it was still her wish to see us, we returned on another day, but though not repulsed as before, we had to retire, as a feast was being given to a company of Brahmins within.

"Well, once again, a few days ago, we had a direct call from the woman herself as we were passing; and soon we were surrounded, not only by a little company of women, with kindly faces, in the midst of whom sat our special friend in the shape of a Brahmin widow; but also a large gathering of men, youths, and children grouped around us, and listened very quietly to some of the most stirring hymns, selected by us, as well as to a plain statement I read them from a little book, concerning the true way of salvation. As we were taking our leave of this company, several of the women from other houses urged us to visit their homes too, which we were only too glad to do, finding new opportunities in the circle of friends connected with each.

"The young native teacher of another school to which we introduced ourselves, came up to our gharree the other day, and asked us to visit his mother (Sassoo), sending a boy along with us to show us the way. Here we had a capital opportunity, a number of women crowding in, while several men and boys seated themselves in the little courtyard. The teacher himself joined us, and graciously granted permission to his shy-looking wife to learn to read, along with another member of the company who had consented to become a pupil."

CHAPTER IV.

EVANGELISTIC VILLAGE WORK.

MR. AND MRS. COOPER, the missionaries at the head of the Society's mission work in Nagpoor, were accustomed to itinerate in the villages around in the cold season, and, upon their inviting Miss Mackay to join their party, she gladly consented. Here again, an extract from one of her own letters will convey the most vivid description to the mind of the reader of such visits.

"Yesterday morning saw us make an early start for 'the district' before daylight. Mr. Cooper, Timothy, and Elisha (mission-helpers) had set out on foot. Take a peep at us as we turn out of the avenue into the road. In front are Virima and a band of the bigger girls, all looking very comfortable in their bright shawls. Mrs. Cooper and I follow, and the rear is brought up by the 'ark' or large coach-like gharree, my tonga, and a bullock-cart for the girls. It was a lovely morning, keenly cold, but so clear and bright that all nature looked glad. . . . Milestone after milestone we passed as we journeyed on,

A BULLOCK-CART.

and still we did not seem to near our purposed place of encampment; for instead of eight miles, it turned out to be fourteen, as our pedestrians found to their cost. . . . Two or three busied themselves over getting ready the morning meal. The others, with all haste, got out the tent-gear, and set to work erecting the same into those wonderful patriarchal tenements, so suggestive of olden times. First, the stakes on which the cords had to be fastened were to be driven into the ground. Just before being reared the tent looks like a folded umbrella, but by a long pull, a strong pull, and a pull all together, it is gradually induced to expand itself generously for the accommodation of the homeless ones seeking its shelter. I have a little Noah's Ark-like tent for myself by way of a bedroom—a little pet it is, with its quaint brown canvas walls figured with a perpendicular coral-like pattern. I cannot say I spent a very comfortable night in it, however, for, do what I would, I could not get warm.

"In the afternoon, we all set out for the neighbouring village to do a little evangelistic work. Mr. Cooper and his assistants went by themselves, to minister to the men, while Mrs. Cooper and the rest of us went to minister to the women. I had fallen behind with one or two of the girls, and this led to our ultimate separation from the rest of the party, as a woman beckoned me to speak to her, and we soon found ourselves surrounded by a group of her neighbours, along with herself, to whom we sang some hymns, and told the Gospel story. Passing on in search of Mrs. Cooper, but not finding her, we again gathered a group around us, and did what we could amongst them. This morning I wandered into the city, and not knowing in which direction to turn, I was looking about me, when I discovered Mr. Cooper surrounded by a little band to whom Timothy was preaching—his sunlit countenance and mild expression giving beautiful emphasis to his words."

Again, "On Sunday afternoon I asked Mrs. Cooper to let me have Virima, the Bible-woman, with me, as well as my usual quota of the girls to help me with the singing, and she was quite agreeable. In passing up the street, we were called by a woman. She wanted to hear us again, as she had 'forgotten what we had told her the day before.' Poor woman! The 'certain strange things' brought to her ears had not been sufficiently grasped by her. She was a woman in very humble circumstances, trying to spin cotton, though her arms and hands were sadly deformed and shrunken. A good many neighbours gathered around, and we had a nice little meeting, which was brought to a close by our telling them we must go farther up the street and tell others what we had been telling them."

So the band of mission workers proceeded, for days and weeks together, sowing the seed of the kingdom by all waters,—sometimes accorded an enthusiastic reception, and at other times scarcely endured. Occasionally they would meet with a band of strolling musicians, who would, however, listen eagerly to their hymn-singing; at other times, they were entertained in the native fashion, in native homes. In one home she was laden with flowers, in another, feasted with sweetmeats. She says: "Another pleasant experience I had when a hymn (wholly unintelligible to me because in Hindustani, and not in Marathi) brought tears into the eyes of a stout woman amongst the listeners, who had been trying to show me that the Koran is the revelation to *them*, as the Bible is to us. I begin to reap the fruits of perseverance in visiting all who call me, be their language what it may, and their motive what it may in inviting me. The bright idea occurred to me, lately, that I could order copies of Gospels in all the different languages spoken around us, and use them in exceptional circumstances. In carrying out this idea, I have been able to give Gospels in Gujerati to the Parsees while teaching them English; in Telugu and Tamil to the Madrasees, and so on, in this way meeting the exigency in some measure, and having an opportunity of 'holding forth the word of life,' to the very mixed population in this centre of the Central Provinces."

Her perambulations among the villages were not always so cheerful or pleasurable. The "rainy days," which come into every life, came into hers at times, and from different letters to friends we find that various mischances befell her. At one time, the wheel of her bullock-cart broke down, so that she was beholden to the kindness of a native gentleman to take her back again to the city. A conversation with this modern good Samaritan revealed the fact that he was a Theosophist, whereupon Miss Mackay seized the opportunity to urge him to examine also, as carefully, the claims of the Christian religion. At another time, the murder of a man and woman in the neighbourhood, by criminals anxious to possess themselves of the jewels of their victims, made her almost afraid to sleep alone in her little bungalow; but the precious words of the ninety-first Psalm reassured her trembling heart. On another missionary journey she was able to succour and comfort a poor soldier's widow, who was proceeding to Bombay with her three children. And sometimes she met with travelling friends herself, who would share with her their refreshments, much to her comfort. She was ever on the look-out for opportunities of doing good, and sowing the seed of the kingdom, whether it were among a group of natives, or among the wives and families of soldiers. She said, writing home once: "We must work in season and out of season,—in other words, to catch men, and not become weary in well-doing, for in due time we shall reap if we faint not." Miss Mackay acted out this precept of our Lord, so that she became known as a seed-sower wherever she went. She was always on the watch for opportunities to win souls.

CHAPTER V.

SOWING BESIDE ALL WATERS.

MISS MACKAY'S sympathies were much drawn out towards the soldiers, and she frequently visited them, in company with some other mission worker. There was much need of evangelical ministrations among this neglected class of the population, as various entries in her journals and letters prove. They drank to excess whenever opportunity offered; and in India, where every glass of spirits is said to be "a nail in a man's coffin," the result may easily be divined. Miss Mackay, writing home on this matter, says: "You will scarcely guess my new sphere of labour. Well, it is among the soldiers at the Fort! The thought crossed me one day, that I would get Mr. Douglas to pay them a special visit, that he might distribute a lot of nicely illustrated magazines I had picked up when in Bombay. It was suggested that I myself should visit them. No objection being raised, the suggestion took root, and I engaged Mrs. Douglas to accompany me some evening." Accordingly, one evening, the two ladies went, and sang several hymns, which so recalled the home-land, that some of the soldiers joined in the singing. The result was that the ladies were asked to come again. Finally, Miss Mackay was requested by the soldiers to hold a special service in the mission church for their benefit, which, though an ordeal to the lady, resulted in good. It was almost impossible to read or talk without interruption at the barracks, seeing that some of the soldiers delighted in rioting and making uproar. Still, much good was accomplished, and some of the men professed to have undergone a saving change, as the result of Miss Mackay's ministrations. It will be seen that these ministrations were needed when we mention that within a fortnight eight poor fellows were cut off by sunstroke—a result chiefly of their drinking habits, added to the intense heat of the climate.

About this time, a younger sister joined Miss Mackay in the mission, and lived in the lonely bungalow (which she had occupied *alone* for the year) with her. They visited the native houses in company, and were kindly and even warmly received. In many of them there was beginning to be a value put on education, and a strong love developed for the teacher. Sometimes they would be called into a house, and requested to read or sing; at others, they would visit homes on occasions of festivity, and ever met with a welcome, for all the people delighted in listening to singing. They could catch ideas better from hymns than from sermons, and these ideas would take root in their minds very frequently, and bear encouraging fruit. We give an extract from her account of such a visit :—" About ten days ago, we had a splendid opportunity of singing Gospel hymns, and telling the story of Jesus' love, to one of the most motley throngs I ever saw. We became the central objects of attraction as soon as we had entered the large pavilion, and the attention bestowed was wonderful. The youthful bridegroom could not read, so there was no use in giving him a book; but several little fellows present carried off small prizes gained

A YOUTHFUL BRIDE AND BRIDEGROOM.

on the spot, by a public exhibition of their proficiency in the art."

Sometimes these domiciliary visits revealed the fact that the master of the house was a decided believer in Christ, and was teaching his wife the way of salvation through Him, though quietly, so as to arouse no bad feeling on the part of his neighbours. At other times, it was discovered that though convinced of the truth of Christianity, the people had delayed and quibbled, until from being very near the kingdom, they had grown hardened and indifferent. The duty of *confessing* Christ had been shirked, and the curse had come upon them—of hardness and impenitence of heart.

Everywhere it is pleasing to find that Miss Mackay was kindly and even eagerly received, while in many cases the people hung upon her words, as if the new and strange doctrines were of such amazing comfort that they could not miss one word. But space fails to tell all the pleasing incidents that might be recounted.

In November, 1882, she returned to Scotland, after five years of work, for a twelvemonth's furlough. During that furlough, she might have made what is generally spoken of as "a good marriage," but she chose to return to her beloved work, for Christ's sake. By February, 1884, she was back in Nagpoor again, and labouring eagerly among the old ties. In what spirit she did so, may be seen from the following:—

"It was my privilege to resume Zenana mission-work here some nine months ago, after a year's absence at home—a year ever memorable, bringing with it abundant opportunities of usefulness, and much refreshment of spirit, apart altogether from the great benefit derived by a renewed measure of health and strength. Never before did I enjoy so much delightful intercourse with Christian friends. After seeking to water dry and thirsty places here for five years, I was 'watered also myself,' and oh how refreshing the showers were felt to be. Never shall I forget last year's memories."

So she continued to labour among the ever open households of Nagpoor and vicinity, until October, 1886, when after eleven years of most devoted labours she was married to the Rev. Johan Ruthquist, a Swedish missionary, labouring at Amarwara, a lonely village in the jungle, about twenty-six miles from Chindwara. Henceforth she helped her husband in his labours among the Gonds or " hill-men," as they are called. It involved some measure of sacrifice to settle down in the lonely jungle, afar from all the associations and friends of her years of labour. The Gonds are known as "timid, truthful, and superstitious. They had about fifteen deities to whom they prayed and sacrificed, and were in addition, devil-worshippers; but they have a strong sense of sin, and of their need of a living sacrifice, and of the shedding of blood. Dark and dense as their ignorance was, they presented a much more encouraging field for work than did the Hindoos, as they had so much less to unlearn, and were so much less self-righteous." So here, also, Mrs. Ruthquist pursued her new avocations, making the mission-house, which was comfortable and roomy, an example of Christian living to the surrounding natives.

But to Mrs. Ruthquist there came now a period of suffering. She had worked longer than the general average of women-workers could do in India, and though tried by climate and other influences, maintained a fair state of health. But her active, working life would not have been perfected had not some kind of suffering come into it. She became a mother, at the little lonely mission-station of Amarwara on the 15th of November, 1889, giving birth to a little girl,

C

whom the parents named Mary Juanita. But this only little one (for Mrs. Ruthquist never had another) died after twelve days, under rather mysterious circumstances. Both the parents and the medical man suspected that the infant had had opium administered to it, as it was impossible to rouse it out of the twelve hours' unconsciousness which preceded death.

This sorrow fell heavily upon Mrs. Ruthquist, but the thought of meeting her lost baby in the land of light and love was a strengthener and comforter to her mourning heart. She began to prove now the truth of the beautiful words, "Work is but one half of life; suffering is the other." Writing home at this time, she says: "I was just thinking that little babes will be restored to us at the resurrection, just as they were when we parted from them; for we cannot imagine that the little body that was laid in the grave will be changed into a big one. The development of mind and body will take place afterwards I think, but like that of a perfect flower, never to fade again."

Mrs. Ruthquist's sister Maggie, who had married another Swedish missionary,—Mr. Danielsson,—was settled near Amarwara, among the Gonds, so that the two sisters could have frequent intercourse. This sister found in her compound one day a forsaken infant, who had been cast away by its mother, who happened to be one of the mission-house servants. The child was named Benjamin, and the two childless sisters resolved to bring him up, between the two houses, training him for the Lord. It was customary for Mr. and Mrs. Ruthquist to ride about to the little villages in the neighbouring country, and teach the Gonds the good news of salvation through Christ,— he preaching and she singing. If we had space to write more at length of the evangelistic work accomplished by Mr. and Mrs. Ruthquist in their journeys up and down the Gond country, it would be seen how valuable and how valued their labours were. Sometimes the heathen listeners would say of Jesus Christ, "*Show Him!*" To this her answer was a Christian hymn, translated into the vernacular, which was explained verse by verse, and which touched the hearts of the people.

In 1892, a mission dispensary was opened in Amarwara, and bodies as well as souls received healing. Here is one of the cases ministered to, which shows in a striking light that the dark places of the earth are full of cruelty. "The other day my husband came in and said, 'I cannot understand how people can be less merciful towards each other than towards their horses and dogs.' Our sweeper's son-in-law had told him of a girl who was lying in a deserted wayside inn, in the greatest misery. No one gave her anything to eat, or took any care of her. She had 'lost caste.' Here one could see what it was to be 'without caste.' John hastened to the poor girl, but the smell where she lay was so fearful, in consequence of her illness, that at first he almost fell down backwards. She was being eaten alive by worms almost, which had made large holes in her head, from whence came this dreadful smell. We called our own servant, and she was carried to our mission-house to be taken care of. I summoned my courage, and went to see her. Never shall I forget the sight. Before we could attend to her sores, her hair, which scarcely deserved the name, was obliged to be cut off as closely as possible, and then John had more than an hour's work injecting disinfecting fluids, and picking off parasites. The girl was extremely exhausted, and began to tremble and complain of hunger before she was cleaned. Our kind old sweeper made as much haste as he could, and comforted the girl, who began to cry, telling her that now she had become quite a new person. Porridge and newly baked bread she ate ravenously. How had she come into such misery? and how old was she? She had been turned out of doors by her husband, because she had eaten something which had been offered to an elephant by all the caste, and since that she had wandered about begging till, in consequence of her wretched condition, every one had driven her away from their doors.

"EVERY ONE HAD DRIVEN HER AWAY FROM THEIR DOORS."

She had then determined to lay herself down and die alone in the deserted inn, and very soon this would have been her fate unless some one had rescued her. She is between fifteen and sixteen years of age, of a slight and womanly appearance. Poor 'Poosiya' (this is her name) is now getting better, and her strength is returning."

Circumstances now began to indicate that Mrs. Ruthquist was to remove her tent from India, though she knew it not. On the 25th of July, 1892, the wife of Mr. Karlsson of Saugor, a brother missionary, died, leaving an infant a few days old, and another child aged one year and eight months. Mr. Karlsson was strongly advised to take the little motherless children home to Sweden, there to leave them with relatives, so, though Mrs. Ruthquist had offered to look after

"THEY CAME TO THE MISSION HOUSE AND WEPT BITTERLY."

the orphans, it seemed best to take them home. He, therefore, wrote to her, asking if her husband could spare her to accompany him and the children to Stockholm. Mrs. Ruthquist was not as strong as of yore; indeed, her friends were apprehensive that she was far too weak for such an undertaking. But she believed that "God's biddings are enablings," and in this faith she cheerily undertook the journey and responsibility. Still it was no light thing to have wakeful, wearisome nights with so young an infant, in her enfeebled state. The intense heat of August in the Red Sea, however, drew on; but the hope of safely accomplishing her errand, and after that, of spending a month at home, in dear old Scotland, sustained her for a while. She wrote a cheery letter on the 29th of August, telling her parents of her arrangements and plans, and saying that she could only spend a month with them as she had made "a sacred promise" to her husband to be "back in India by Christmas, God permitting."

She had, however, overrated her strength, which now utterly failed, and on the 4th of September she was compelled to take to her bed, trusting to get rested while Mr. Karlsson looked to the two children. But the weakness grew and intensified, until within twelve hours she became unconscious. She lay thus for another day, when about 5.30 P.M. on the 5th of September she sank to rest, without a struggle or a groan. "She had reached the haven, while her friends were still far out at sea." Her last message to her husband was written on a luggage label, inside a parcel, which she had forwarded to him from Bombay. It was this:—"Jesus Christ, the same yesterday, to-day, and for ever." "They which live should not henceforth live unto themselves, but unto Him who died for them, and lived again."

> "My times are in Thy hand;
> My God, I wish them there;
> My life, my friends, my all I leave
> Entirely to Thy care."

"I'll always trust in Thee."

Mrs. Ruthquist was buried at Suez, having gained the Promised Land of Heaven, somewhere near the point where the Israelites crossed the Isthmus to gain their Promised Land. When the native women at Amarwara heard of her death they came to the mission-house, and wept bitterly that she had not been allowed to die among them, so that they might have had the privilege of going to lament over her grave.

> "Of all the thoughts of God that are
>   Borne inward unto souls afar
>   Along the Psalmist's music deep;
>   Now tell me if that any is,
>   For gift or grace surpassing this,
>   He giveth His beloved sleep."

MRS. BOWEN THOMPSON.

Mrs. Bowen Thompson's
MISSIONARY WORK AMONG THE DAUGHTERS OF SYRIA.

CHAPTER I.

BEGINNINGS.

IT has often been said that "The child is father to the man," and the saying was never more truly exemplified than in the case of the subject of the present sketch. From "Recollections" contributed to a memoir by a surviving sister, we find that from her early childhood, Mrs. Bowen Thompson was distinguished for seeking to do good to others. "The love of God as it dawned in the first years of her childhood, was especially manifested in the exercise of a strong and simple faith." Her family motto, "Dare and persevere," was changed into the Apostolic one, "I can do all things through Christ which strengtheneth me," and bore good fruit in daring all things for God.

According to the testimony of those who knew her best, she was religiously disposed from her very childhood, so that sometimes thoughtless companions taunted her with being "a little saint." Certainly, her study of the Bible and Prayer-book indicated principles and leanings of no common kind. To this was added a keen interest in the discoveries of remains and monuments in Bible lands, casting light on Bible prophecy. The discovery of the Rosetta Stone by Consul Salt, in Egypt, led the sisters of the home to study the lore of the Pyramids. While in her teens, she was busy, up to the extent of her opportunities, in doing Christian work of one kind and another, among all with whom she came in contact.

On attaining the age of womanhood, she was invited to work on behalf of the Syro-Egyptian Mission by Sir Culling Eardley. Her association with this Committee led to an acquaintance with Dr. James Bowen Thompson, who had for years devoted his professional talents to the service of the Syrian Mission. He had opened, and personally conducted, the British Syrian Hospital at Damascus from 1843 to 1848. The acquaintance ended in marriage, and after a short residence in London the young couple proceeded to Syria, and settled at a little place near Antioch, where Dr. Bowen Thompson owned some property. Here, she grew to know more of the ignorance of Eastern women, and opened a school for them in her own house. This labour went on for about eighteen months, and then, on leaving for the seat of war in the Crimea, to which Dr. Bowen Thompson seemed irresistibly drawn, the little school was left behind with a Christian native teacher, and several Armenian converts, who continued to meet for prayer and worship each Lord's Day. As they bade a tearful "good-bye" to the little band of scholars and converts, it was not easy to foresee the future.

THE CITY OF DAMASCUS.

It seemed a strange step, to leave Antioch and its neighbourhood for the seat of war. But Dr. Thompson had gained much knowledge of Eastern epidemics and disease, and felt eager, considering the extreme need of medical aid in the Crimea, to place his services at the disposal of the English Government. Before the commission from Lord Panmure could reach him, he and his wife were on their way to the seat of war. They arrived at Balaklava, but almost immediately Dr. Thompson was stricken down with the malignant fever which raged among the troops, and was put on board the steamer engaged in the conveyance of invalids to the military hospital at Scutari. Here, the rigid military rules forbade admission to the suffering invalid, as his commission had not yet arrived, so making him to be, in the eyes of the military authorities, only a civilian. After some delay, however, through the intercession of Dr. and Lady Alicia Blackwood, permission was granted to admit the fever-stricken man. The boon, however, came too late; he was admitted to the hospital in the closing days of July, and seemed at first to go on well, but by the 5th of August he had passed away. The poor widow followed him to his grave, accompanied by the nurses and some of the medical staff. "His grave was under a spreading tree, commanding a fine view of the Bosphorus and Constantinople."

After this, Mrs. Bowen Thompson returned to England, and found a congenial home with her sister and brother-in-law at East Coombe Park, and while with them learnt to be "a succourer of many." The dreadful Indian Mutiny broke out in 1857, and her heart bled for the forlorn widows returning from India. Monetary assistance, clothes, widows' weeds, and clothing for children, were all needed by those who had left husbands and fathers in the far East, as victims to the vengeance of Sepoy rebellion. In these, and other works of mercy, Mrs. Bowen Thompson served her generation. Her biographer finely says: "As the physician's widow, she now entered upon her last term of education in God's school. This, to all her previous training, was the needful complement, ere she could prove a capable and sympathising teacher of husbandless isolation and bereavement. She had now her commission from God. She now heard, as it were, His voice calling for some tried and pitying hand to pour into the wounded spirit the balm of a Saviour's love, to hush the widow's sobs and the wail of orphans clinging to her knee. The occasion for the application of all her past experiences now immediately dawned."

In 1860, the bloody massacre of the Maronite Christians by the Druses of the Lebanon district of Syria attracted attention and sympathy. Lebanon and the district round Damascus had been deluged with Christian blood, and the Druse soldiers did their best to slay every male among the Maronites, from seven to seventy years of age. It was, in truth, a religious war of extermination, carried on by fanatical Druses against the sect of Christians known as Maronites.

Without a brief explanation of these circumstances, it may be difficult to understand or appreciate the condition of things which attracted Mrs. Bowen Thompson's Christian sympathies. The district of the Lebanon is peopled chiefly by Druses and Maronite Christians. The latter, a hardy, industrious race, are Roman Catholics; but the former profess no religion. The Druses were masters of treachery and intrigue, and especially hated the Maronites on account of their numbers and prosperity. They framed pretences for war, and engaged the willing help of their Turkish rulers to aid them in the work of extermination. The Maronites, who were armed and trained in self-defence, brave in war, and industrious in peace, needed their time and labour for the cultivation of their land, and consented to give up their arms, on conditions of amnesty. They were

BEYROUT.

then entrapped, in this helpless condition, into the forts of their enemies, where they were murdered by thousands. After the massacres were over, a commission of the Allied Powers investigated these atrocities, and thus reported, "There were eleven thousand Christians massacred; one hundred thousand sufferers by the civil war; twenty thousand desolate widows and orphans; three thousand Christian habitations burned to the ground; four thousand

Christians perished of destitution; and ten million dollars worth of property destroyed."

Mrs. Bowen Thompson worked for the Syrian Temporal Relief Fund in sending out stores and clothing; but her own experiences of widowhood and bereavement suggested to her that now was the time to arise and engage in a work for the poor, sorrowing women and girls of Syria. So she started for Beyrout, while just emerging from an attack of illness, in October, 1860. Perhaps prudence just at that period would have been the better part, for immediately upon her arrival at Beyrout she was laid low with an attack of rheumatic fever. During this illness she experienced the greatest sympathy from the European residents, including Lord Dufferin and his mother. At length she was able to sit up, and walk about the corridors of the hotel on crutches. As soon as she was able to mount a donkey, she rented a house, and removed thither, intending to commence her work of mercy among the bereaved widows and sufferers.

We cannot do better than relate the commencement of Mrs. Bowen Thompson's work, as detailed herself in a letter to a friend.

"You will remember the sanguinary massacres which decimated the male population of the Lebanon and Damascus district in 1860. Suffice it to say, the Mohammedans and Druses made common cause for the destruction of the Christian population, and their bitter enmity often provoked strife. The Maronites and Greeks of the Lebanon, who fled for refuge to their Mohammedan rulers, were betrayed, and the men delivered up to the sword. The order at Hasbeya was that every male from seven to seventy should be slain.

"Thus thousands upon thousands were butchered. Those who escaped to Damascus were, in a few weeks, also cut down by the Turks, Druses, and Kurds; their houses were rifled and burnt, and their widows and orphans abandoned to all the horrors of flight. Stained with the gore of their husbands and sons, the sound of the murderer's sword still ringing in their ears, crowds of these helpless widows and children fled distractedly, they knew not whither; some to Tyre and Sidon, but the greater part to Beyrout, the seaport towns of Syria. When tidings of these fearful events reached Europe, England sent large contributions in money, food, and clothing. Many of my friends, and the members of my family, took an active part in organising various sources of relief; and as it had pleased God that during the Crimean War I should be one of the many who suffered bereavement, it was but natural that my heart should respond to the widow's cry. Then, too, the happy portion of my married life which I had spent in Syria had enabled me to acquire some knowledge of the language, as well as of the ignorance and degradation of the women. Therefore, as a widow caring for the widow, I felt specially called upon to try and alleviate their distress, and make known to them the only balm for a broken heart— the love of Jesus. My first effort was to meet with suitable premises for an Industrial Refuge, . . . and I commenced in December, 1860, with thirty women and sixteen children. Within a week we had above two hundred under our care.

"Our gates were besieged by applicants clamouring for admission, saying, 'Even if you cannot pay us for our work, let us come and sit and listen, for our hearts are sad.' At this juncture I received not only liberal aid, but cheering intelligence that our friends in England had formed themselves into an association called 'The Society for the Social and Religious Improvement of Syrian Females.' At first my heart often died within me at the squalor, noise, and misery of these poor people. Ignorance of the truth, and deeply cherished revenge characterised the greater number of the women. Even the families of priests would say, 'We are like the cows; we know nothing.' When, however, their Christian teachers unfolded to them the Bible, they would sit at their feet in rapt attention, exclaiming, 'We never heard such words.' 'Does it mean for us women?' 'Now, we will always sit here!' While some few blessed God for the privilege of learning to read His Word. Women as well as children commenced with the alphabet, but such was their avidity to learn the daily text and portion of hymn taught by dictation, that in a short time the Bible was in their hands, and the songs of Zion rose up to heaven, instead of their former imprecations and idle talk. Groups of women being taught by their children now met the eye, and in their miserable abodes, as well as at school, the Bible was read, and the teaching of the Holy Spirit sought in prayer."

At the time of Mrs. Bowen Thompson's arrival at Damascus, twenty thousand refugees were crowding the khans (inns) of the city, huddling into rooms with no openings but doors, and no conveniences of life. The women were glad to get work at a piastre (about twopence) per day at even road-mending, so absolutely destitute had the cruel massacre left them.

Mrs. Thompson procured two or three excellent native assistants to help in cutting out work for the women, and in teaching the children, of whom she had a school numbering one hundred.

CHAPTER II.

SCHOOL WORK.

BESIDE these occupations, Mrs. Bowen Thompson found opportunity to visit the sick and dying at the hospital—an extemporised institution, adapted from a house of a former European resident. From the patients in this building Mrs. Bowen Thompson heard many sorrowful tales. A young woman, with three little children, one of whom was dying in her lap, had seen her husband and three fine boys hacked to pieces before her eyes. In another room was "a fine-looking old woman, with the hand of death plainly to be seen upon her brow. She had been brought in only the night before. After propping up her pillows, to make her comfortable, I tried to say a few words to her about her soul, and asked her, 'Was she ready to die?' She shook her head, and clasped her poor shrivelled hands with an air of deep sorrow. I went out to see if there was any one who could read some message from God to her soul. Daond, the cook, said, 'I have my Bible, but the people will not listen to it. I must not read it; they will be so angry.' I said, 'Never mind, God will not be angry.' He looked delighted, and fetched his Bible. I told him what to read. He read part of John xiv., and such texts as chap. iii. 16. I soon saw that he was not only acquainted with his Bible, but had been taught of God. He constantly bade her say, 'Lord Jesus, save my soul! Cleanse me from my sins! Give me Thy Holy Spirit!' The poor woman repeated the words after him, while the Greek nurse stood over her, calling out at each petition, 'Say Jesus, Mary Joseph, have mercy on me!' The poor old woman seemed at a loss, but soon gave her mind to what the young Arab cook was reading. Oh! what a grief it was to me not to be able to speak to that poor dying woman. Then came the assistant-doctor, who said, 'This woman is dying; send for the priest.' I could only pray that Jesus, the High Priest, might be with her, and absolve her from all her sins. . . . I do earnestly hope that this poor woman may have received the message of Christ's finished work to her soul. She, too, was a Damascene, and had been very rich. She saw her husband hacked to pieces, which so affected her heart that she had been ill ever since."

After ministering to the destitute refugees in the necessary matters of food and clothing, Mrs. Bowen Thompson determined to open, to use her own words, "English, industrial, ragged, and evening schools in Syria." She looked to the Committee of the Syrian Relief Fund for supplies of clothes, books, working materials, and money wherewith to pay the workers and teachers. The magnitude of the work would have overwhelmed a weaker woman, and appalled one with less faith. But Mrs. Thompson was not an ordinary woman. The "Deborah" of nursery days—for by that name she was hailed often by her brothers and sisters —proved equal to daring and doing great things for God. She rented a large house for her purpose, and opened it for the miserable sufferers whom she sought to serve and save. We must here quote a letter of hers to the Syrian Relief Committee detailing her general plan, so that our readers may understand her beginnings of work. She says, writing to her helpers at home:—

"In one room we shall gather the children; and

Saada Barakat, the excellent young widow from Damascus, whose husband was killed, and herself and child left destitute, is to be the teacher of this Ragged School. Her salary is 200 piastres per month, with food and clothing.

"Second room—*Industrial Department* for women and girls, under the superintendence of one of the Damascene widows.

"Third room—The depôt for receiving and giving out the work of the Anglo-American Committee, under the care of another widow from Damascus, who has lost her all, and will also help in the housekeeping.

"Fourth room — *Stores from England*, which, I trust, like the widow's cruse of oil, will not fail so long as there is an empty cruse to be filled. Mr. Consul Moore is much pleased with the evening school for teaching the young men Arabic and English. I have engaged a master for about fourteen pounds per annum. We are only waiting for you to send us the books. Arabic Bibles and Testaments I look for from the British and Foreign Bible Society; English spelling-books, adult reading, Scripture portions, map of Syria, etc., I greatly long for, and trust they will be sent rapidly."

Mrs. Thompson soon set her poor women to work, but the demand both for garments and workers quickly exceeded the supply. Speaking of this she says:—

"The door was besieged by some fifty poor women, all entreating to be taken in, but I had to be firm and refuse them, and shut the door. We are well supplied with work from the Relief Committee. The Rev. Dr. Thomson at once got me a number of warm jackets and clothing to make up for the people from Diel el Khamar, as they wish to send them from

Beyrout as soon as possible. So now we are hard at work. The Relief Committee will pay me one piastre and a-half per day for each woman, three piastres for two, or if need be three helpers; but I shall have to pay the teachers about thirty shillings per week. The teachers are delighted with their work, and even these few hours have made a great change in their expression. One poor woman came in during a pelting storm, with nothing but an under-garment and a few rags to cover her, while her sickly babe was barely covered with wet tatters. I took from our bundle of old clothes a little night-gown and frock, and we dressed the crying babe, to the great delight of all the women. When we get our boxes, and can afford to give a few garments to these poor people, it will be a boon indeed."

At the end of 1860 Mrs. Thompson secured a house in the suburbs of Beyrout, so spacious and convenient as to afford schoolrooms and work-rooms, with sleeping accommodation for the orphans. Thirty widows from Hasbeya formed the nucleus of the working-school, and, in addition, the poor women were taught habits of cleanliness and household management. This adult school was always opened with Bible-reading, prayer, and a hymn, either repeated or sung by the whole assembly. The hymn, "My faith looks up to Thee," was a great favourite with the women, and they were soon able to sing it in Arabic. She also found it necessary to open a girls' school for the upper classes; for families who had previously sent their daughters to the French Sisters of Charity preferred to put them under the care of the English lady who taught Protestant principles, and were prepared to pay good fees for the privilege, provided they were allowed to continue their study of French.

MRS. BOWEN THOMPSON'S SYRIAN SCHOOL AT BEYROUT.

Mrs. Thompson, therefore, made arrangements for such a school, and engaged another teacher, and, as she expected, she found the income from this branch to be a great aid in the support of the widows and orphans.

Very soon she had to convert an old stable into an additional class-room for adults, and before two months had gone she opened an infant school, which, within a week, received ninety pupils. Yet the work grew, for she had to throw another set of outbuildings into one large room, to accommodate a school for young women. She could not have set on foot so many branches of work had not a sister from England, and that sister's husband—Mr. and Mrs. Mentor Mott—joined her, resolved to work also for the good of the destitute people of Syria. In consequence of their home in England having been burnt down, they resolved, rather than rebuild, to imitate Mrs. Thompson in spending and being spent for the poor Syrian sufferers. A younger sister—Miss Lloyd—had already been helping her for some time. So that now there were four individuals out of one family hard at work in the self-denying enterprise of feeding the hungry, clothing the naked, and instructing the ignorant. Surely such an example is very rare! And the undertaking grew and prospered, until Mrs. Thompson herself was amazed at its magnitude. She says of it:—

"When I began, amidst great discouragement, I had not the slightest idea how large and how rapidly the work would grow, and when I now look at the schools as they stand, I own I marvel at what the Lord has wrought in little more than two months and a-half. Not a single woman or child has been asked to come here, but I have had to select, and now we have 65 women, and 110 children, and here for the present we must stop, for, as it is, the care of this large flock completely exhausts my strength and time. Added to this, refugees from all parts come here. From dawn till dark, notwithstanding all precautions to admit none but our own women and children, others make their way into the garden, and follow me from room to room entreating for work and clothing. . . . I had almost forgotten our Sunday evening class, when some of the parents and brothers, as well as our workers, and their friends, come. The few who can read sit round the tables and read verses in turn, after which Selim (a teacher), reads a chapter, and explains it. Many questions are asked, and then we close in prayer."

In addition, Mrs. Thompson opened a laundry, which was largely supported by the officers of Her Majesty's fleet, then lying in the roadstead. By this means some dozens of women were provided with occupation and maintenance. The stories told by these women were very bitter. Here is one which could be multiplied tenfold : " She told the sad tale of her experiences in the massacre, and how she had stood up to her knees in blood, while the Turks stripped her of her ornaments ; one even attempting to cut off her finger for the sake of the diamond ring ; another cutting her neck with a knife, in taking away her pearl necklace. Then, of their sufferings at the castle, exposed to the burning sun, with scarcely a rag to cover them, hungry and thirsty, and how some Mohammedans who were once their friends brought them bread and meat which, when they had tasted, made them sick, and her mother and darling child died in convulsions from the poison the wretches had put into the food. Others had also died from the treacherous act. Sometimes at the schools, the only ones who could be prevailed upon to sing the hymns were the little children; the women would say, 'their hearts were too heavy.'"

In July, 1861, the people of Zahleh expressed a strong desire to have an industrial school opened there. One chief promised to give his house for a school, and his daughters "to be Mrs. Thompson's servants." The people themselves surrounded Mrs. Thompson in groups, begging her to open a school without delay. Mrs. Thompson opened a school here, and it became a prosperous institution.

CHAPTER III.

ENCOURAGEMENTS.

IN 1862, we find Mrs. Thompson writing: "Our schools have been useful in giving an impetus to the education of females, and I quite expect in the next generation it will not be the reproach of this country that the women are degraded, idle, and ignorant. The thirst for instruction is extremely great, and were it not for the love of money, and the pernicious influence of the priests, *education*, and not merely instruction, would be deemed essential, and sought and paid for by the people themselves. But it is ours to sow in faith."

Again, "I had no money in hand for my poor widows. They were without food; I could not taste my own dinner. I went up into my own room, and besought the Lord to give me the means of helping them. While yet in prayer, the excellent Prussian Consul called to tell me he had opened a soup-kitchen, and would give a meal every day to fifty of my poor women. Jehovah-Jireh.

"Last week, when the anxiously anticipated box of Bibles arrived, the women and children in our schools were eager to possess this treasure. When I told them that I could only let them have them on their paying a part of the cost, many voices called out, 'Kadesh, kadesh!'—how much? how much? 'Ten piastres' (1s. 8d.), I replied. A sorrowful look came over many a bright young face; but when I proposed receiving the amount in weekly instalments of one penny, more than twenty at once gave in their names.

"In our women's school, which numbers a daily attendance of fifty, there are some in whose hearts the Holy Spirit's influence is clearly at work. Lately some of these widows have had very severe persecutions. The owner of the houses of some of the women actually turned them out of the house because of their prayers. One of the women, Mart Mosa, of whom I have told you before that the Lord had opened her heart like that of Lydia, had a prayer-meeting one evening every week at her house. At the request of the women, I have allowed them the use of the great hall every Wednesday. Our two Bible-women have been very hard at work, and what I have told you of the prayer-meeting may be traced to their great but unobtrusive work."

In May, 1862, H.R.H. the Prince of Wales paid a visit to the schools at Beyrout, and was extremely pleased. On his arrival near the outer premises, he was astonished at being greeted by the children, who stood in long rows inside the garden singing "God save the Queen" in the Arabic tongue. At the Prince's visit next morning, he asked to hear them sing, read, and recite in the Arabic language, and further inspected the needlework, being particularly attracted by the specimens of gold embroidery executed by the women. Next day, he sent Mrs. Thompson a present of twenty-five Napoleons, accompanying the gift with a large order for gold embroidery.

Writing in 1863, Mrs. Thompson says: "Not only have we under Christian instruction the children of those who were butchered in cold blood, but the children also of those by whose order, if not by whose hands, multitudes were slain. Yes; the Druses, the very sound of whose name, not a twelvemonth since, excited such a commotion in our schools, are now sitting side by side with these same girls, learning the same Gospel, and singing the same hymns of praise. For the last four months we have had the two daughters of a Druse Sheik who was condemned to death for his evil deeds, but was afterwards sentenced to banishment instead.

"Mr. Selim Bustros (a Syrian gentleman), came last Thursday and examined the women's and children's schools for nearly two hours. I cannot tell you how astonished and delighted he was. He had known many of the Hasbeyan women before the massacre, and was amazed to find them in this school neatly clothed, educated, and in a better mind. He heard the girls read a chapter from Exodus in Arabic; Luke in English; also Arabic hymns, geography, arithmetic, the first class in fractions on the black board. They recited various pieces in English, and then he examined their writing, both Arabic and English. He spoke to the girls, both individually and collectively, and expressed his delight at what was being done in these schools, and urged the girls to be diligent and punctual in their attendance. He further said that he never expected to see his countrywomen so enlightened, and begged I would remove the schools nearer to the Greek quarter (more aristocratic), that the families round might send their daughters. He said he would do all he could to facilitate our getting a good house at a reduced rent, and offered to build a school at a considerable reduction."

Mrs. Thompson records, now and then, encouraging instances of spiritual good among the old women pupils. Here is one which is too interesting to be passed by:—" The blessing our Women's School has been to some who have not been able to learn to read, in spite of their long-continued efforts, is now evidenced in Shehene's mother. She was with me before the school opened, and is the most aged of the widows. She has been sinking for some time, but would not see her danger, and was angry when anyone spoke of death. She was very fond of the school, and it was touching to see the old spectacled grandmother, bereft of her husband and all her sons, sitting on the mat, and learning to sew, or repeating her A B C or text of Scripture. When we called to see her yesterday, she said : ' Dear lady, I bless you for that school ; I cannot sleep at night for oppression and cough, but those words I was so long in getting by heart ' (I think it was three months ere she could repeat them correctly), ' are always sounding in my ears : " Come unto Me, all ye that labour and are heavy laden, and I will give you rest."' It was affecting to see the old woman sitting upright on her mattress on the floor. She said she was a great sinner. I asked her, did she not know the hymn, ' Just as I am '? Her countenance lightened up, and then she joined Shehene and myself, with our faithful Gebour in singing it. 'But there is one hymn I love better,' said she, 'which we used to sing at school,' and then she sung—

> 'My faith looks up to Thee,
> Thou Lamb of Calvary.
> Saviour Divine.'"

Towards the end of 1863, Mrs. Thompson was prevailed upon to set up schools at Hasbeya, a place in the Lebanon, some few miles from Beyrout, and in the midst of the district decimated by massacre. The refugees who had lived at Beyrout so long, and profited by Mrs. Thompson's sewing-classes and teaching, were compelled to return to their ruined homes in Hasbeya, or forfeit the small allowance granted by the authorities. But it seemed impossible for them to return to their ruined homes, broken-hearted and alone, to commence re-building. Mrs. Thompson says: "Many of the women urged me to transfer the Women's School to Hasbeya, and to open a Girls' School there, so that they might continue to enjoy the spiritual and temporal advantages to which most of them had been strangers when they came to Beyrout." Before deciding this matter, it was necessary to visit the district of Hasbeya and the neighbouring villages. Accordingly, she did so, and the record of her own impressions, as related in her letter home, is most interesting.

"At the little village of Ain Kamyreh we found our tent prepared; but instead of getting any repose, crowds of women and children gathered round us, but oh! so fearfully ignorant. They scarcely seemed to know that God made them; and in answer to our question, 'What would become of them after they are dead?' they replied, 'How should we know? We are women! we are Arabs!' Georgius (a teacher) spoke very plainly with them, but none could answer the simplest question. 'Who was the first man?' 'In how many days had God made the world?' 'How should we know? We are like the cows; we know nothing!' The missionary and native preacher were engaged in talking with the men; and when we had separated after dinner, most anxious for a little repose, the women and children came again, and said: 'Would we open a school for them?' They begged Georgius would again read the Gospel to them; and squatting down on the ground near the tent door, he read Luke xv., and applied it to them. Their looks were riveted, and even the children listened with the greatest attention. . . . We then proceeded to Hasbeya, where is a very fine temple of Baal; indeed, the region of Dan abounds in idolatrous temples."

At Hasbeya, they found ruins of cottages and shops—indeed, there was scarcely a house or a roof left; while in some cases, the dirty, half-starved women were trying to re-build their homes with their own hands. "Amid the masses of ruined houses sat an aged widow on a low stool, with a little earthen pot of charcoal before her. Her hands were folded on her knees, and she sat motionless as a statue. By her side was a little sort of wigwam, not high enough for her to stand upright in, and under this miserable shelter the poor widow sleeps, bemoaning the dead, and without hope for the future."

Having finally secured the goodwill of both Mohammedans and Druses, and taken the names of fifty girls who promised to attend school, Mrs. Thompson engaged a room, ordered it to be whitewashed, and the floor covered with mats, and then appointed one of her trained girls as mistress. Further, she engaged such of the native women, as

workers for wages, who could knit stockings, and understood making garments. These articles would find a ready sale at the monthly fair, which was held in the neighbourhood.

At other villages where she stopped on the return journey, with her party, Mrs. Thompson was entreated to open Industrial Schools. In some cases, where the ladies of the village promised protection, she consented.

In the spring of the following year Mrs. Thompson and her friends made a tour through the Holy Land. A little incident which happened to the party in the plain of Esdralon illustrates the dangers of travel in that land. The incident is recounted by Mrs. Thompson's sister, Mrs. Mott, in her book, "Stones of Palestine." It appeared that, in crossing the plain of Esdralon, the party were benighted, so that the guides lost their way, and a party of Arabs from the notorious village of Hattin offered to lead them. Mrs. Mott says: "We remounted our horses, led by these mysterious strangers. There passed a peculiar call from mouth to mouth and from place to place—something thrillingly frightful. Elizabeth overheard their conversation, and told us we had fallen into bad hands. One party was evidently urging on another to some deed, to which he replied, 'I am afraid.' 'Why is that man afraid?' asked Elizabeth. 'Is he afraid of the wolves? I am not afraid of them.' The men, finding she could understand them, said the 'call' was a watchword to let their people know that the strangers were coming. It was midnight when we reached Hattin, wending our way down the rough mountain pass. Here, a number of men, above a dozen, were lying down. They started to their feet, threw off their Arab cloaks, and made a movement with their weapons. One of our guides now had a close consultation with their chief, and, meanwhile, Elizabeth, with her usual tact, had asked for their wives, and, though it was so late, a nice young woman came out. Elizabeth, who had previously inquired her name, now addressed her familiarly as 'Ischi,' and told her we wanted some 'lebban' (a delicious, thick, sour milk), and begged her to give us some. After some parleying with the men Ischi brought us out butter, or, more properly, buttermilk, 'in a lordly dish.' Now we knew that we were safe, for having once shared their hospitality they are bound to defend—not to injure."

The year 1864 witnessed the most encouraging progress in all the schools, and the purchase of the sites and buildings was completed. The total number of schools in Beyrout was eight, and in these four hundred pupils of different ages and both sexes gathered regularly, while at some important Lebanon villages, such as Hasbeya and Ashrafia, other schools were in working order, with a total of about two hundred scholars in daily attendance. Most visitors to the Holy Land heard of these schools, and visited them. Among other visitors Canon Tristram was shown over them, and published a most interesting account in his journal. A few sentences from this volume will convey to the reader a truer conception of the abiding value of Mrs. Thompson's work than can any extracts from her own papers, and with them we close this chapter.

"I must not omit to mention what was by far the most interesting to me in Beyrout—the female schools established and conducted by Mrs. Bowen Thompson. Here, nearly four hundred native females — married women, girls, and infants — are receiving a sound, useful, and thoroughly Christian education. Nowhere has the experiment of female education in the East been tried with more success, and nowhere has it been conducted on more uncompromising and thoroughly Christian principles. Nor is it merely orphans and outcasts that are taken in, and orphans such as those from the massacre of Hasbeya received and clothed—a very large proportion are the children of the wealthiest families in Beyrout, who pay for their education at a liberal rate. All the races of Syria are represented."

CHAPTER IV.

CLOSING DAYS IN SYRIA.

THE account given by Mrs. Mott in Mrs. Bowen Thompson's Life of the funeral of the wife of a Greek houri (priest) illustrates the success won by the Gospel among the Syrian people almost more than anything else can do, and will be perused with interest by our readers:—

"Mrs. Thompson and I mounted our horses and rode to the houri's house, which stands in a large mulberry garden. What a scene presented itself! In front of the cottage, stretched on a low bier, wrapped in dark clothing and covered with a veil, lay the wife of the Greek priest. More than one hundred women were seated on the ground near the bier. Among them was one of our Bible-women, who was speaking in a low tone. The three daughters were seated at the head of the corpse. They rose, and most affectionately greeted their beloved teacher. Mrs. Thompson spoke a few words. Such a holy calm pervaded the whole. The men were assembled at the back of the cottage, but the houri, on hearing that the lady had arrived, came up and spoke to us,

BIBLE-CLASS OF MOSLEMS.

and then stood a little way off. There were no large candles, and no bemoanings. Our teacher, Georgius, opened his Bible and read very impressively John xi and parts of John x. and xiv. He then made an earnest, simple address on the resurrection from death to life, consequent upon the resurrection from sin to holiness, making a personal appeal to each one present; he then repeated their favourite hymn, 'My faith looks up to Thee,' the women all repeating it after him, and concluding with the Lord's Prayer. It was a most solemn service, and would have been striking even at the funeral of a Protestant. Never before has such a service been attempted at the death of a member of the Greek Church, that member being the wife of a priest, who was present the whole time, and who cordially thanked Mrs. Thompson for all her kindness."

Long ere this, Mrs. Bowen Thompson and her co-workers had so won their way among the Syrian peasantry that visits, instruction, Bible-readings—all were eagerly welcomed, as well as temporal succour. Schools had multiplied until many important villages and centres became supplied with these institutions; so that the number had increased far beyond what she had at first intended, or hoped. Boys' schools, girls' schools, infant schools, orphanages, Sunday schools, "Olive-branch" schools, Moslem boarding-schools, blind schools, and a school for cripples, were all in working order in Beyrout and the Lebanon. It was wonderful whence the supplies came. Moslem boarders paid, it was true; but all the profits, after deducting expenses, went to the support of other institutions and their teachers.

Mrs. Thompson had a wonderful tact for choosing workers; and having chosen a young lad or girl to assist her, she gave that assistant a proper course of training in her Normal Training College, from whence, after the period of training was completed, each was appointed to branch or village schools. Most of these institutions were supported by her own means, and those of her family. Friends and travellers who visited the spot, and saw for themselves the self-denying work carried on by Mrs. Thompson and members of her family, assisted with donations, which were always welcome; but still, for the regular means of support, her private fortune was laid under tribute. In the whole history of missions it would be difficult, if not impossible, to find another instance of this kind.

As a final effort, schools were established at Damascus; for even in that city the longing for instruction had entered, and the Moslems entreated for a school to be opened in which their daughters might obtain a thorough education, embracing English, French, needlework, and other accomplishments. Of course, they had to pay for this privilege—which they were perfectly willing to do—and the school fees went toward the support of Arabic schools for the poor. By opening this higher-class school first, Mrs. Bowen Thompson secured the good-will and co-operation of the Moslems, and was, consequently, able to open other schools for the poor and needy. Not only so; but at a conference held before the establishment of any school at all in Damascus she secured their co-operation, as also that of the Jews, as witness the following statement from her journal:—"It has been agreed upon, that as the rich were contending *the poor ought not to pay*, that they should do so for them; and I proposed that for every pound they should have the privilege of sending four children for one year free to our Arabic school, and this, I am glad to say, meets their objections. In this way, several Jewish children have been already adopted—

four little ones for one pound. May a rich blessing attend this plan."

In 1868, the last full year of her service in Palestine, Mrs. Thompson records that teachers had been trained in the College for "two schools in Damascus, three at Zahleh, two at Ain Zahalteh, two at the 'Olive Branch' at Ashrafia, one at East Coombe, two at Musaitbeh, one at Jerusalem in Bishop Gobat's School, and one at Cairo, with dear Miss Whately." Last of all, the schools at Damascus were founded, which she says "may be regarded as our crowning mercy." And, day by day, numbers of pupils sought admission, far above the capacity of either teachers or buildings. Very soon the Prince of the Hauran district presented a petition for the establishment of a school in one of the Giant Cities of Bashan; but Mrs. Thompson had to tell him that her hands were so full she could not undertake more. Yet it was with sorrow and regret she said this; for in the cities of the Hauran district the ignorance was so dense that poor people, widows even, in the direst poverty, actually paid their priests heavy fees to secure two feet square of standing-room in heaven after death. And to such a people the entrance of God's Word would have been the coming of that which "giveth light."

In 1869, Mrs. Thompson suffered from illness induced by overwork and responsibility—an illness which was really the precursor of the end. The following summer was one of weakness and prostration; but even while in bed she occupied herself with reports and operations of the school-work. She said once to one who sat by her: "Notwithstanding my great weakness, I have never one instant lost my peace of mind, or the sense of the presence of Jesus."

In September of that year she returned to England, and went to a sister's home at Blackheath, reaching there on the 7th of October. But though apparently benefited by the voyage, she continued sinking so low that before many days the physician pronounced her condition hopeless. This decision was communicated to her; but it did not disturb her mind, nor stop her thoughtful arrangements for her Syrian schools. In one of her last prayers she used these words: "And now, Lord, let none of those who know me, and none of those who love me, ever think of me as going through the grave and gate of *death*, but through the gate of *glory!*" Her marvellous quietness of mind astonished all who saw her; it literally seemed as if angels bore her company. Mrs. Thompson's sister, writing of the end, says:—"Several times her feet seemed to touch the very brink of Jordan. Her large bright eyes intently fixed, her hands stretched out, and looking upwards, she said faintly, 'Glory be to the Father, the Son, and the Holy Ghost. Jesus! Jesus! Rest! Rest! Arise! Amen!' As the last midnight hour of the Sabbath was tolling out its solemn sound, she deliberately crossed her arms upon her breast, and resigned her spirit into the hands of Him who gave it, and while in the very act of commending her soul to Him, she entered into that rest which remaineth for the people of God."

She passed from earth to heaven on the 14th of November, 1869, leaving many behind who would, doubtless, follow her.

Here we must close. Of the sorrow of friends, the bitter lamentations of the Syrian orphans and pupils, we can say nothing; but of Elizabeth Maria Thompson it may safely be said that she shall be held "*in everlasting remembrance*" in Syria.

> "With wisdom, grace, and love divinely blest,
> She raised the fallen, shielded the oppressed.
> The blind she led to touch the Word and see;
> And healed the strife of creeds by charity.
> Damascus mourns her—Hermon's daughters weep—
> Their 'mother in the Lord' has fall'n asleep.
> Her native land hath claimed her mortal part;
> Jesus her soul; but Syria hath her heart."

DR. MARY McGEORGE.

Dr. Mary McGeorge,

MEDICAL ZENANA MISSIONARY TO INDIA OF THE
IRISH PRESBYTERIAN MISSION.

CHAPTER I.

EARLY DAYS—CONSECRATION AND TRAINING.

MARY McGEORGE was the seventh child and eldest daughter of James McGeorge, Esq., J.P., of Newry, County Down. She was born at Newry, on the 30th of April, 1850, but in 1860 the family removed to Carnmeen House, a picturesquely-situated residence, three miles from the town. From her earliest years she was thoughtful and studious—never idle, but ever helpful, and always seeking for something to do for the good of others. We are told that she busied herself in visiting the aged and sick near her home, and established an evening Sabbath school for the benefit of the children of the labourers on the place, as well as for those children of neighbouring families who were willing to attend. Mr. McGeorge was a very intelligent man, and encouraged his children in their intellectual pursuits and studies, while the cultivated, gentle mother ably seconded him; so that the tone of the home-life conduced to, and fostered in the members of the family, intellectual life and activity. In all this Mary shared, growing by its means more fitted, as years rolled on, for the great work which God meant her to do.

A time came when Mary saw before her what she had long desired—a definite work on behalf of Christ and His Kingdom. It came about in this way. The late Rev. Dr. Fleming Stevenson was a greatly esteemed friend of her father's, and as he passed hither and thither, in various ministerial or other errands, he became, from time to time, a much honoured guest in the home at Carnmeen. Previous to the visit which led to a decision to work in Zenana missions, information concerning that branch of work in connection with the Irish Presbyterian Church Missions in India had been eagerly sought for; and so much did this information touch the heart of Mary McGeorge, that several Auxiliary Missionary Societies were established in the neighbourhood of Newry, mainly by her instrumentality. She acted as secretary to these Auxiliaries, and by the distribution of missionary letters (for the Mission had no magazine in those early days) kept alive the public interest in the work of the Zenanas. Her own efforts roused, she by degrees drew into active co-operation many who now serve the cause of missions with whole-souled devotion. What, then, could be more natural than that she should become, in far-off India, an accredited and earnest worker? She had no particular home ties; her heart was in the work, she was active, healthy, energetic, and, beneath her outwardly quiet manner, enthusiastic. She had received a good education, the last year of her school-life having been spent at Clifton, under Miss Millington, principal of a school for ladies there, and this made it comparatively easy for her to enter upon a university career, with a view to a special profession.

Yet she had other and higher qualifications. Those we have mentioned would not, of themselves, afford justification for entering upon a life of toil and self-sacrifice in Zenana missions, although we all admit that scholastic training and educational acquire-

THE HOME AT CARNMEEN.
(*It was here that Miss McGeorge decided on her life-work.*)

ments are indispensable. It required much love, sympathy, and a single aim, in humble dependence upon the Holy Ghost, to lead others out of darkness into the marvellous light of the Gospel. All these qualifications were possessed by Mary McGeorge, and she waited humbly and prayerfully for the call. That call came, and in this wise. In one of Dr. Stevenson's visits to the home, he believed he saw in his friend's eldest daughter one who was in every way fitted to labour successfully among our neglected Indian sisters. He spoke his thoughts, explained the nature of the work, and asked the mother (the father being dead) if she would consent to part with her daughter. Then, turning to the daughter, he asked if she were willing to leave home and friends for Christ's sake? The response was immediate; the call had come, and the prepared heart responded fully, so that from that moment, Mary McGeorge was devoted to the service of the Zenana missions of her father's Church.

In pursuance of her consecrated purpose, her application to be appointed Zenana medical missionary was forwarded to the Missionary Committee at Belfast, and received by them on the 7th of November, 1878. The Examining Committee, before whom the candidate appeared, handed in a satisfactory report, and she was unanimously accepted.

The decision having been definitely made, no time was lost in entering upon the needful studies. Just here, it may be useful to remind our younger readers of the difficulties which existed in those days in regard to the intellectual rights of women. The medical course connected with colleges was not yet thrown open to women. The idea was very novel and very distasteful that women should have access to the same medical classes as men. "There was no precedent for such a course;" "the thing would not work;" "the male students would not stand it;" "let women stick to their own sphere;" "they will lose refinement and delicacy;" "they have not the nerve;" "there is no room for them;" "let them become teachers, or hospital nurses, or anything rather than doctors." These, and many other unkind things, fell to the lot of all women who sought medical training during the time of which we write. Still it may not be amiss to refer to these things, if only in order to show how many difficulties and prejudices had to be overcome by any woman who longed to enter the noble profession of medicine. But after many struggles, the day dawned when no one would think of hinting at the exclusion of women from the medical profession, for it had come to be recognised that they were richly endowed with all the needful qualities of intellect, nerve-power, and of judgment.

Eventually, fully-equipped schools of medicine were established, and to one of the chief of these—the London School of Medicine for Women—Miss McGeorge betook herself, her name appearing in the register of that Institution as having entered in October, 1879. Her course of study embraced the usual subjects, and in two of these, Chemistry and Surgery, she passed with honours.

As preliminary to this medical training, she had passed, previous to her London curriculum of study, in Latin, German, English Literature, and Geometry at the University Local Examinations, held in the Hall of Queen's College, Belfast.

Her career in London was uninterrupted, and unusually successful. She worked diligently, never missing a class or a lecture, and passed every examination with credit, her four and a-half years' course ending in 1884. Mary McGeorge was not one of those who offer on the Lord's altar that which costs them nothing. The best of her life, her power of brain, and her heart's love were freely offered to Him whose she was, and whom she served.

CHAPTER II.

THE NEW SPHERE OF WORK.

WHILE awaiting her appointment, Miss McGeorge acted for six months as house surgeon to the New Hospital for Women, Euston Road, and while gaining valuable experience there, became a valued worker. In May, 1884, she passed her final examination in Dublin, for the Licentiateship of the King's and Queen's College of Physicians, and also took the L.M. diploma.

On the 31st of July, 1884, Miss McGeorge started for Vienna, for a course of special study. But she left England in somewhat weak health, and being prostrated with severe illness, after a few weeks was compelled to return home to England by easy stages. Early in November of that year she arrived at the new family home at Buxton, her mother having removed from Ireland to that town.

During 1884, and the earlier months of 1885, Mrs. McGeorge's health steadily declined. She had spent much upon her daughter's medical education, and her longing desire to see Mary as a worker in the mission-field appeared far from being gratified, as, day after day, she showed no signs of returning strength.

Meantime all Mary's spare hours were spent in devoted attendance upon her much-loved mother. The thought of shortly leaving that mother, perhaps never to see her again in this world, was a sorrowful one, but God had decreed that the separation should take place prior to Mary's departure. During September the mother "fell asleep," and her remains were laid to rest in Fairfield Cemetery. So, across the threshold of Miss McGeorge's life-work lay the heavy shadow of bereavement, saddening her heart as she bravely stepped forth to her service of love for the Master, in a strange and distant land. The great link which held the young missionary to this country was now broken in the inscrutable Providence of the all-wise Disposer of lives. Mrs. McGeorge had, as we have already seen, longed to see her daughter enter upon the life to which she had so cheerfully dedicated her, but this was not to be. The mother departed to see "the King in His beauty," and the daughter set out to carry into execution the dearest wish of that mother's heart.

A valedictory service was held at Rosemary Street Church in Belfast, on Tuesday, the 10th of November, 1885, to take farewell of Dr. Mary McGeorge and Miss McDowell, on the eve of their departure for India. Dr. Fleming Stevenson was there, and addressed the two women consecrated to the work in language affecting, cheering, and tender, as he could well do. Doubtless he remembered that early scene when Mary consented to devote herself to the work in response to his inquiry and urging, and he and all who heard him had full hearts.

The missionary party, of which Miss McGeorge was a member, sailed from London in November, 1885, on board the P. and O. steamer *Nepaul*, and reached Bombay, *via* the Suez Canal, late in December. Two of the Presbyterian missionaries met the party at Bombay, so making the young beginners' first experiences of India pleasant and free from difficulty. *En route* to Ahmedabad—a city which was to be the centre of her work for the next few years—stoppages were made at Surat and Anand, to familiarise the newcomers with the distinctive mission operations carried on at these centres, and give them a foretaste of what lay before them. First impressions are generally striking, and every detail possesses interest. Miss McGeorge had a faculty of observation, and her descriptions of places, person, and customs are always vividly pictured.

Her first letter deals with initial impressions of mis-

BRAHMINS OF SURAT.

sionary operations at Surat. She says: "You will have heard of the safe passage of the *Nepaul*, P. and O. steamer, by which we arrived. It was uneventful —the usual thing: stormy in the Bay of Biscay— enjoyable in the Mediterranean—very close in the Canal—very hot in the Red Sea—cooler in the Indian Ocean, or perhaps I should say the Arabian Gulf. Everyone was delighted to anchor off Bombay. I was glad to see Mr. Taylor and Mr. Shilliday, who met us.

Having been on the Continent makes one feel less foreign to the open houses and matted floors, and all

PARSEE CHILDREN.

that kind of thing. . . . It is not possible to say yet how I like India, because we are not yet in our own home. We stayed a week in the Zenana house at

Surat. The mission work is getting on well, and as it was holiday time we saw some phases of it that we should not otherwise have seen. A number of Parsee girls came to see us, and stayed to afternoon tea. It was interesting to see them, and to hear from them about their study of English and other subjects. I believe that Parsees are most difficult to get at however. They receive instruction in the Scriptures willingly, but are slow to be acted upon; still they learn, and some are Christians, but not able to declare themselves so. It is easy to understand how hard it must be for them, when they would have to leave their homes, and be outcast for the sake of Christ, for there is no place to which they could go."

Again, she adds: "However, there is a great deal of underground work going on, and it may be that some day they will come out in numbers and have each other's support. . . . I was down in the dispensary a few times."

Again, "Mr. Shilliday has charge of the printing-press. The books and tracts they print have a wide circulation, so that a great deal of good is being done in that way." . . . "I also visited a Mohammedan lady with Miss Roberts. The house seemed very bare, but I was told this uncomfortable abode was the residence of one of the first families. We then visited the Armenian Church—it was a ruin, a home for bats. We then went to a native school—three small rooms, with the boys sitting on the floor like tailors. I think I shall find India and my work will prove most interesting."

On the 6th of January, 1886, Dr. Mary McGeorge arrived at Ahmedabad. The two ladies were met by Mr. Taylor, a missionary coadjutor already resident there. Her verdict was that "Ahmedabad was a

fine city, flourishing and very different from Surat." The accompanying illustration of the Zenana Mission House in Ahmedabad, gives a good idea of the general style of dwelling occupied by Europeans in India. She says, "Bungalow is a term applied to one-story dwellings, but as the illustration shows two stories, the more dignified name of 'house' is properly applied to the mission residence. An upstair room is an advantage, inasmuch as it protects from malarial ground influences, and gives one the chance of getting any occasional breath of wind there may be. During the day, however, the upper room becomes a strongly-heated furnace, from which one flees, owing to the lack of a verandah, similar to that on the ground floor. The dark rolls, visible under the edges of the verandah roof, are 'chico,' or blinds made of very narrow thin laths; these are let down in the daytime to exclude the glare and the hot wind. Some people prefer hot wind to none at all, and, therefore, leave all the doors open, and banish 'chico'; but under these conditions the glare is very blinding, and must in time injure the eyes.

"On the ground-floor there is just one long apartment. Of this a quarter is screened off to form a bedroom; the remainder is divided by a folding-screen into a sitting-room and dining-room. Behind the sitting-room is a tiny apartment, which does duty as a surgery.

"All roofs are tiled, or should be, and in the picture will be seen the ravages made thereon by the sacred monkeys. Troops of monkeys hovered in the neighbourhood, and from time to time made a general stampede over the house, scattering tiles in every direction. These animals—a dozen at once—would rush across the sitting-room, tear up the stairs, and down again, while the occupants of the sitting-room would calmly gaze at them, and, indeed, would not attempt to interfere with their vagaries. Now and again a scorpion would be found by the wall, close to where a member of the mission band had been

SACRED MONKEYS.

sitting, and sometimes it would creep about on the floors at night, making its presence known by striking the floor with its tail, keeping rhythmic time to its own steps. Occasionally, too, there would be an alarm in the compound (or yard) on account of the presence of an invading snake, creating alarm, and even terror.

"The doors must be kept open at such times as the monkeys make their inroads, and this is chiefly during the rainy season, unless the deluge of rain compelled them to close doors; but in this case it would be very dark, as there are no windows in the Mission House. It is not so very much cooler during the rains, but rather a different kind of heat—'a steamy, muggy, kind of atmosphere,' certainly one which would be extremely unhealthy."

Before passing to the account of Miss McGeorge's work, it may be well to remark that there is much quiet, underground work of a religious character among the natives of India which cannot very well be tabulated, but is none the less *real*, and which must tell in time to come, if it only has a fair chance. Such work is literally like "seed sown by the wayside." This view is strongly held by missionaries of all the evangelistic Churches who have laboured there. Though comparatively few outward results appear from various forms of missionary labour, there is an undergrowth of belief in the Christian religion which would spring up and bear abundant fruit, but for the "fear of man." There are many secret disciples; and if by some work of the Holy Spirit these secret disciples could be brought to band themselves together, a bright day of Gospel light and life would dawn upon India. The following extract from a letter refers to this question:—

"AHMEDABAD, *20th April*, 1886.

"—— is in heart a Christian, but he is waiting for baptism in the hope that his wife will also come out. He says she believes in Jesus, and reads the Gospel of St. Luke every evening. What makes them both hesitate is the caste persecution they would have to endure. The Hindoos are a timid race, and what they would have to pass through is, in any case, formidable. He says he knows about forty Hindoos in Ahmedabad who believe in Christ, but dare not avow their belief. Perhaps some day a nation will be born in a day."

Another interesting case is also referred to by Miss McGeorge, presenting very nearly the same difficulties. Our readers will be thus enabled to understand some of the peculiar trials of mission life :—

"AHMEDABAD, 2nd August, 1886.

"—— has brought his wife to read, and he wished her to attend the Female Training College, but she was afraid that she might be made a Christian, and therefore has not gone. The struggle within himself as to whether he may have courage to be baptised still continues; but I think he is growing stronger in the faith. He is naturally well inclined. From time to time I give him a tract on the subject, or lend him a book."

The next extract refers to the case of a young Mohammedan, a student at the Mission High School. He went into the schoolroom where a young class was being taught.

"Presently in walked a young Brahmin, a student in our High School. I asked him what he wanted? He said, 'Only to see the class taught.' We invited him to remain. We sang 'I have a Saviour,' and he joined in it. Then followed prayer, after which he salaamed, and said he was going; but I persuaded him to wait. The Bible lesson was on 'The offering of Isaac,' so that pointed to Christ, and I spoke seriously to him. He said that he did not think baptism was necessary, if we kept the commands of

Christ. I told him baptism *was* a command of Christ. They all stumble at baptism, because it seems such a decided step. He promised to come next Sunday."

In this way we think it will be quite easy to detect that the leaven of the Gospel had made its way into native minds; but in how large a percentage of cases this assent of the head was followed by the allegiance of the heart it would be very difficult to say.

CHAPTER III.

HEATHEN MANNERS AND CUSTOMS.

AHMEDABAD was wholly given up to idolatry in many forms. We find that among the high festivals of heathenism in the district, could be reckoned that of Krishna's birthday. The people also worshipped serpents, and observed certain days as sacred to them. The process of worship mainly consisted, however, in drawing serpentine lines in the sand and indulging in feastings. The Gujerati Hindoos seemed not to mind how many objects of worship they had, and the greatest uncertainty might prevail over the facts and origin of a superstitious custom; nevertheless it was observed all the same. Some extracts from Miss McGeorge's letters will prove these statements.

"To-morrow at 4 A.M. begins the anniversary of Krishna's birth, and to-day is also a great holiday. The people have been bathing in the Sabarmatti river for purification, and they will spend the remainder of the day visiting the temples, perhaps eight times. They only look at the idol, and give money to the priest."

Miss McGeorge also describes a mourning celebration among the Mohammedans. "Last Saturday was the great Mohammedan festival of *Mohurrum*,— a festival in honour of Mohammed's grandsons, Hossein and Hossan, who died in one day, fighting for the cause. The observance or festival is called 'The Tabut.' We had a splendid view of the procession. About 150 'tabuts' were carried along on men's shoulders at intervals of about a minute. These 'tabuts' are like huge toy mosques, made of wood, and covered with gold and silver tinsel. Some are really expensively got up. Then a wooden elephant was dragged along on wheels, and also a wooden peacock. The streets were densely crowded along the route, and Sepoys preserved order. The people here were quiet, but in some other places there were riots. The 'tabuts' are supposed to be thrown into the Sabarmatti river, to appease the gods, and favour the ghosts of Hossein and Hossan. I believe that they cast in only poor little 'tabuts,' and reserve the good ones for next year. However, they are nearly all carried down and sprinkled with the river-water, which is sacred. Inside some of the 'tabuts' there are fruits and representations of various figures. Over each 'tabut' a canopy was borne. Men followed beating their breasts and dancing wildly. Although it is a Mohammedan festival, the Hindoos take as much part in it as their former conquerors."

Miss McGeorge tells us her personal experiences of the climate. In September, 1886, she narrowly escaped a sunstroke.

"October is the most trying month of all. However, the season has happily not yet affected my health, but the climate is very trying all the same. One never feels buoyant here; always inclined to

ZENANA MISSION DISPENSARY, AHMEDABAD.

succumb to the heat and its attendant evils, so that it is always working against the elements. If one admits the fact that it is impossible to get through so much in a day as at home, and rests contented, one can do pretty well. It certainly is an impossibility to study as at home. Night study is very unhealthy, and the days are just melting.

"The other morning, walking a few steps to the Ghardi from the Dispensary, the sun struck my back, and I felt sick for a day or two, and had a great headache. The hardened natives go about unhurt. Most of the men have an umbrella; the women have not, and I suppose custom has inured them."

Again, "One month of work at the Dispensary is over, and some grave cases have come. It is said that Lord and Lady Dufferin will visit Ahmedabad next month. The day that the Duke and Duchess of Connaught landed was kept as a general holiday."

About this time Dr. Fleming Stevenson passed away to his reward, leaving behind him a gap which could not be filled. Miss McGeorge thus laments him:—

"We are all shocked to hear about the death of Dr. Stevenson,—so suddenly called away! His place *may* be filled, but there are few so enthusiastic and of such a kind, gentle, thoughtful disposition. What an amount of work he crowded into his life! He said once he 'did not like to lose an opportunity of work because, though life might be prolonged, each opportunity came but once.'"

Miss McGeorge held to the opinion, in common with other missionaries, that the time is coming when native workers will do the work that foreign missionaries are now doing in India. Writing on this point, she says:—"Here all Churches look forward to the time when foreign missionaries will not be needed at all, but the whole Church will be managed by the natives themselves. But I believe that day to be far distant."

We get just a little peep at her medical work. "I may be said to be in full swing now. This is my routine of work. Every day from 8 to 10.30 I am at the Dispensary, and attend from 75 to 80 patients. Then home to breakfast at 11 A.M., and very tired. Pundit for two hours, or his wife for Scripture lesson and sewing. At 3 P.M. a cup of tea, study till about 5.30; walk; dine at 7 P.M.; at 9 we have prayers, then bed. This is the usual routine."

Again, "My medical work proceeds daily as usual. I get patients from every caste; I have had to put up a notice that no man is to come without permission. Yesterday there was rather a hubbub because a man came with his little boy. I let him in by a different door, and made him wait behind the curtain. He said he had been to many doctors, without benefit, and he therefore came to me. There is a sad lack of proper ideas in this country. Most things are just exactly the reverse of what they should be."

About this time Miss McGeorge paid a visit to Borsad,—a town which was the first station occupied by the Irish Presbyterian Church. It lies in the elevated table-land of Gujerat, at about 1900 feet above the sea-level, and is connected by rail with Bombay and Baroda. The population numbered about 13,000, and presented an interesting field for mission labour. Here she was summoned to attend the Ranee, who was ill at a village close by. But, after a few days' work and visiting, she was back in Ahmedabad again, eager to take up her duties.

CHAPTER IV.

LIFE IN AHMEDABAD.

IT will be needful to describe Ahmedabad before going further, so that our readers may be more fully acquainted with Miss McGeorge's work in that city, the city itself, and its position in the Gujerat district.

The city of Ahmedabad is the capital of the district, and is situated on the east or left bank of the river Sabarmatti. It was formerly one of the largest cities in India, celebrated for its commerce and manufactures. Silk and cotton fabrics, articles of gold, silver, steel, enamel, mother-of-pearl, lacquerie ware, and fine wool-work, were all manufactured there. With the rise of the Mahratta power, however, Ahmedabad became the scene of repeated struggles between the Mahrattas and the Mussulmans, whose power began to wane. From this period its prosperity declined; it was captured by the Mahrattas in 1755, and again by the British in 1780. The British soon gave the town back to the Mahrattas, who held it until it finally came into the hands of the English in 1818, during the rule of Warren Hastings. At present, the city is flourishing; it contains a population of over 116,000 souls. It has a large and important station on the Bombay, Baroda, and Central India Railway. It is the seat of important silk manufactories, and has two cotton-mills worked by steam-power.

The city was founded by Ahmad, grandson of a ruler styled Wajeh-ut-Mulk; who chose a site occupied by a community of the Bhil race, whose predatory habits were the terror of the neighbourhood. He resolved to create a new capital, and this he did, by using up the materials of a conquered city, compelling all its former inhabitants to follow the spoils of their temples and dwellings to the uninteresting and unhealthy site on the banks of the Sabarmatti. The agriculturists are Kimbi, Rajputs, and Koli; while many of them are also skilled weavers. Some of their social customs are very peculiar. For instance, the Hadna Kimbi tribe, when a suitable husband cannot be found for a girl, marry the poor girl to a man already married, obtaining previously his promise to divorce her as soon as the ceremony is over. This being done, the girl is afterwards given "Natra," which is the second and cheap form of marriage, to any one who will wed her. Such is the lot of many a poor native girl; sold into the bitterest slavery, without a word of her own upon the matter. What would our own girls say to this? The humblest and hardest-worked maid-servant in the British Islands is a queen in her own right compared with her Hindoo sisters! thanks to the religion of Jesus.

The principal architectural attractions of the city consist in heathen temples—some of which are of great beauty. The external dimensions of the great mosque are 382 feet by 258 feet, and it is said to be one of the most beautiful mosques of the East. Ahmad Shah and his queen lie buried there.

Writing in some of her depressed moments, Miss McGeorge says: "Sometimes our race seems short, but it is long enough after all. As it is said in the hymn, so I feel, 'I would not live alway.' Life is bearable because we know it has a glad termination. ... Yet, in this country, the heathen around seem happy enough; but this is the happiness from ignorance. They do not think much, and are content to take the hours as they come. It is only the civilised

HINDOO TEMPLE AT AHMEDABAD.

folk who have the pain of deep thought; so true is it that 'knowledge increaseth sorrow.'"

Miss McGeorge tells us, here, how she spent her first Christmas in India among the people whom she taught. The experiences were somewhat different from those of home and the home-land.

"Our Christmas-tree went off capitally. It was a babul tree with thorns that conveniently held the presents and the candles. There were about one hundred and fifty little native children, and perhaps as many grown-up folks—relations and friends—and a few Eurasian and East Indian children."

At the commencement of 1887, she paid a visit to Mount Abu, a hill health-resort and a celebrated mountain of western India, between five and six thousand feet in height. She tells us of some noted heathen temples built upon the sides and platforms of this mountain height, known as "Jain temples." As one reads her description of them, one can realise very fully how the natives of India are "wholly given up to idolatry." She says that one temple was "built by two brothers, rich merchants, about the end of the eleventh century, and for delicacy of carving and intricate beauty of detail, stands almost unrivalled even in this land of patient and lavish labour." Another temple built by a rich merchant prince, about 1032, is one of the oldest, as well as one of the most complete examples of Jain architecture known. The principal object inside the temple is a cross-legged figure of the god Parisnath, seated cross-legged in a little cell, which cell is surrounded by a court-yard and a double colonnade of pillars, forming an immense portico. Outside are about fifty other little cells, just as would be seen in a Buddhist monastery.

Europeans resort in large numbers to Abu, where, owing to the great elevation, the atmosphere is much cooler than in the scorching plains below. It is the favourite spot with missionaries stationed in the Gujerat district, and going to Abu is known as "going to the hills."

Miss McGeorge found many Parsees among the dwellers in that district, and they were invariably apt pupils in all branches of education, but she almost as invariably discovered in them a spirit opposed to the doctrines of Christianity. We quote from her own account:

"The Parsees take on European civilisation more readily than any other of the peoples of India. Would that they would also take on our Christian religion, but that they reject. I do not know of one convert from amongst them in Ahmedabad."

She says, in a letter dated the 13th of May, 1887: "Your letter reached in time to add its weight of influence to that of others, requiring me to fly the plains. We left Ahmedabad on Monday, the 9th, at 10.20 A.M., and reached Abu Road Station at 5 P.M. Here we found conveyances awaiting us—two ponies, a chair, and a 'dandy.' In the dandy (a hammock on poles) one is obliged to recline, and in the chair to sit bolt upright; so Miss M'Dowell and I took each mode alternately. The coolies deposited us occasionally on the road, and refreshed themselves with water and a pipe. Eventually they set us down in a compound, and seemed indifferent to any pressure until a lady emerged and directed us here. Here there are red roses! It is so delightful to see home flowers again! For the first time since leaving Ireland, I feel cool and comfortable, and can write and study without feeling such action to be a distinct effort. One gets tired with so much conscious cerebration. One can live at Abu. At Ahmedabad, one forces one's-self to exist, and to perform one's duty in spite of a temperature of 110 F. in the shade. It has reached 115 F. this week, down in those lower regions. In Surat, the temperature is not so high, and they have not the (hot) furnace wind we have at Ahmedabad.

"In each side of our railway carriage, instead of a window, there was a tatté, which, dipped into water, kept the air cool. This tatté, a species of miniature mill-wheel, is made of grass, and we have to give it an occasional turn.

"Abu is a beautiful place—a mass of hills crowded almost to the summit, crags and boulders, winding mountain paths, etc. A great many people stay here; their time is altogether taken up with amusements, and we see little of them."

The next letter gives us a description of a visit to a heathen temple at this elevated health resort.

"We visited the Dilwarree temples yesterday. If I remember rightly, they are eight hundred years old. They nestle at the foot of the hills, and, it is said, took fourteen years in building. The cost of excavating their sites alone is said to have been £560,000. They are, of course, typical Jain temples. On the flat roof are numerous little domes. Inside, there is a central sanctuary, and around, a square of little cells, fifty-two in number, each containing one, two, or three idols in white marble, sitting cross-legged, and wearing that look of imperturbability common to Buddhist deities. These temples are considered to be next in splendour to the Taj Mahal, at Agra. They are erected on the site of a temple formerly dedicated to Siva and Vishnu, and the founder, Bunul Sah, a Jain merchant of Anhilusana, purchased the site from the Ruler of Sirohi by covering the required ground with silver coin. The building cost eighteen millions of rupees. The second temple was founded in the thirteenth century; the other two, which are much inferior, being only about 400 years old. The pillars inside are all of white marble, and are beautifully carved in small figures."

Miss McGeorge returned to her work in Ahmedabad much benefited by the change of air and scene. She soon resumed her correspondence.

We get a little insight into the self-esteem and pride of the Brahmins in the next letter. The "Brahmins are gentlemen," according to their own opinion.

"AHMEDABAD, *8th August*, 1887.

"This month is a great holiday time, especially with the Shravaks. One-third of the population of Ahmedabad is composed of Shravaks, a sub-division of the Vanias. One boy told me yesterday, 'We Vanias and Brahmins are gentlemen, and we do not mix with Kimbies and Dherds.' So I told him that the Kimbies and Dherds would get into heaven, and they, the gentlemen, would be left out."

The Stevenson Memorial Fund was raised by the Irish Presbyterians for the establishment of a native pastorate in the Gujerati district, and from Miss McGeorge's testimony it seems that some of these men were most exemplary in their conduct. She says: "There is a native Christian in the Anand district who contributes a tenth of all his substance, so setting a good example. Then at Bhalay, a native evangelist named Nathu has given a bell for the church, in memory of his little daughter. If they show the grace of liberality in this way, it will augur well for the future of the Christian Church in India."

CHAPTER V.

MEDICAL WORK.

"AT the Dispensary, the people like to get the tracts and Parables explained to them by the Bible-woman, and they say: 'We want to understand everything! tell us all!' and they ask leave to visit the Bible-woman's home. She is very good at explaining the Bible, and *somjavos* them well. This word means '*to cause to understand*.' In Gujerati, the fewest possible words are used, and a great deal is left to be understood. For instance, 'What are you doing?' is properly '*Shoon thumming kurro cho*.' One can omit '*thumming*' altogether, and ask only '*Shoon kurro cho*.' Then again, the same word stands for both to-day and to-morrow—*katte*. Another strange peculiarity of this tongue is that they always say 'No' when we would say 'Yes.' House-wives may be interested in hearing how floors are scrubbed over here. Well, they deluge the floor with water; in this they wade, with skirts gracefully tucked up, and walk in a stately fashion, or slide as if rinking. No soap, of course; much loss of time, and little good is the result of these proceedings. We shall be glad when all this graceful rinking is over, and we emerge as from a second deluge, resuming our normal life once more."

Miss McGeorge says in another letter: "I am busy at work again, and the Dispensary is getting full once more. At present I am trying to open a second dispensary in another part of the city—if possible in the Mohammedan quarter. Mr. Taylor has some inquirers now, and I trust they may go on to baptism. One sees so many go to the verge, and yet stop short, that one cannot but feel doubtful. And yet we must go on with such ones as perseveringly as if we knew that they would take the final step. I have three women of the Vania caste who come to me to be taught, and I do hope that all three will yet be Christians. They are all inclined to be so; but whether they will break away from caste remains to be seen."

In her dispensary work, Miss McGeorge was always assisted by a Bible-woman, and a native dispenser. While both she and her assistant were busy putting up medicines for the body, the Bible-woman was talking and reading to the waiting patients, thus supplying healing for the soul. It may be wondered at that Miss McGeorge could prescribe for her patients without being perfect mistress of the language; but she had acquired it partially, and it must be remembered that missionaries in general make a beginning with "stammering tongues," rather than hold back until they have obtained linguistic facility. The following letters deal strictly with dispensary work in 1886-87.

"The dispensary now begins at seven in the morning, and until ten, and very often eleven, there is a constant stream of patients. It was impossible to limit the number to forty; when they appear, one has not the heart to send them away, especially when they come from long distances. They come from Baroda, and from up-country, and naturally wish to return the same day. I am so thankful that our Bible-woman is so capable, and that we have such a truly earnest, sincere, Christian worker. Her heart is in her work, and it is quite evident that she has the one pure aim of teaching the women about Christ. The other morning she sung a hymn, and one young woman is particularly anxious to learn to sing it. A patient paid a friendly call a few days ago, and to

MISS MCGEORGE'S BIBLE-WOMAN.

ASSISTANT AT DISPENSARY, AHMEDABAD.

turn her thoughts to higher things than her physical pain I took up the Elementary Catechism and asked her a few questions. As of course she could not answer them her curiosity was aroused, and then it was easy to lead on the conversation. When I told her that God knew everything, she eagerly inquired, 'Does He know about my pain?' and when leaving, she asked anxiously, 'Was I pleased to see her?' I said I was, very much, and told her to come again. Just now, a lady, a Hindoo, from Ahmedabad came in for treatment. They do not grudge coming any distance for relief. A native doctor came with her. She had been under his care for a time.

"Medical work is interesting at all times, but particularly so in this country where there is so much ignorance about the commonest ailments; at the same time I should not feel half the interest in it were it not for the mission aspect of the work. It is a great comfort to be able to point them to Him who can heal the sin-sick soul. There is no limit to the openings in this country; but then, to undertake half the work that is waiting would need a very large accession to our ranks.

"Sunday last I was called to Nariad to see a patient. She was a Nagar Brahmin—a Brahmin of the Brahmins—and a widow of about thirty-six years of age. She lay on a cot on the verandah in the inner court. She was suffering great pain, and although her sisters and other relatives tried every means they could to afford her some relief it was of no avail, so at last they sent for me, as the native doctor could not attend her. I did all that the circumstances warranted, but I wished very much to get her up to Ahmedabad to some relatives so that I could see her again, as she requires constant care.

It transpired that a widow of her caste must spend the first two years of her widowhood in the house, and can under no pretext depart from this strict law. In ways such as this, one's work is baffled, and the suffering of the patients lengthened. Her son, who is very intelligent, accepted two little books in Gujerati and promised to read them. I hope they will send for me again."

Again, she tells us: "There is an entertainment to be found in the dispensary known only to the initiated. That is the effect of the strong ammonia bottle. Some women who have been permitted to smell the bottle to cure their headaches, ask that their stranger friends may do the same, and advise her to take a good smell; which she generally does, and is, in consequence, rather overcome by it—this effect being anxiously looked for and hailed with shouts of good-natured laughter by the friends, in which the sufferer joins heartily. This big smelling-bottle is known well in many of the villages, and people have walked miles just to smell the bottle, their friends have told such wonderful tales about it.

"The women I am most interested in are the village women. They are very simple in their manner, and have such implicit faith that they believe by drinking one bottle of medicine they will be cured of all their diseases, no matter how serious they may be. Then they listen so attentively. The story of the Gospel seems to go straight home to them, and they receive it, and believe it with great joy. One morning three women came, and after their bodily ailments had been treated I sat down to talk to them. I told them I had something to say to them. They replied in their simple direct manner, 'Speak, sister!' After telling of God's love to sinners, and His sending His Son to die and suffer for us, I saw the tears flowing down the faces of two of the women. I talked to them for some time, and when I stopped they pressed me to go on and speak more. On going away they asked if they might bring me some butter and milk the next time.

"Another very poor woman, who had walked a very long distance, after listening to the Gospel for the first time, was so pleased, that on going away she took an egg out of her basket and gave it to me, saying, 'You have told me good news to-day. I am poor, that is all I can give you in return.' These are just one or two instances of the way in which the women receive the message we have to give them, and there are many such. The dispensary work is very cheering, and opens the hearts of all the women to listen to the Gospel as nothing else can.

"One very miserable woman came, because, as she had only daughters, her husband considered her an encumbrance no longer to be borne. So she did not know where to go, or what to do. She has got some work now, and looks happier; but as her health is quite restored she does not require to attend the dispensary, and she seems very sorry to stay away.

"It is a great step in advance that these heathen women will sit quietly listening to Christian teaching, and even discuss it intelligently. It speaks well for the lessening of prejudice that their husbands and brothers will read the little books some of the women take home, instead of prohibiting another visit where teaching subversive of their own religion is given. In one or two cases the patients did not return when they had a book given them, so that now they are not offered them, but get one when they ask. Sometimes a patient says, 'Give me a book; everyone has read the last one I took away.' They are wonderfully grateful for the treatment of their illnesses, and now and again give a small donation, so as to pay for medicine for others.

"Of the three Vania women who came to me for instruction, only one remains. The first and most promising has removed to another town, where her husband has a post. I tried to induce her to be baptised before leaving, as she understands quite clearly the way of salvation; but, although she admitted the duty of receiving the outward sign, and of making a profession of her faith, she said she could not face the persecution that would follow. She said she would continue to read the New Testament, which I think she can now understand, as she is well acquainted with 'Peep of Day,' and Barth's 'Bible Stories,' and knows the First Catechism and part of the Second. As a reward for saying the First Catechism without a mistake, I gave her the 'Pilgrim's Progress,' with which she is much delighted. It may be that, as her light increases her faith will become stronger, and she may yet be numbered among the members of the visible Church. Her husband, I am sorry to say, has so long trifled with conviction, that now he professes that baptism is not necessary—that he can be saved without it. The second inquirer never came regularly, although her husband was led to believe she attended twice a-week. But she went elsewhere, and, at last, fled secretly, and threatens, if brought back, to put poison in her husband's food. This is one sad illustration of the baneful effects of child-marriages, and is by no means a rare one. The third still comes, and brings a younger brother with her. She has invited us to go to her house, which we intend doing very soon. Her husband is a postmaster, so that they are very respectable; and he, of course, is educated, and anxious that his wife should learn more. She tells me that her husband studies the Bible, and believes in it. There are many such

COURT OF A ZENANA.

even in Ahmedabad, and if only one amongst themselves could be raised up to lead the way, I have no doubt that numbers would flock to the leader, and avow their faith in Christ."

Miss McGeorge sums up some of the results of

Zenana and medical work among women, as follows—especially as it regarded every-day learning.

"A number of Parsees came one afternoon to the Zenana bungalow, and took part in some sewing. One of them stitched as neatly as any machine could do. They sang a number of hymns very nicely, accompanied by the harmonium. They sang in English, and some of them speak it very well indeed, especially G——. She reads a good deal, and on asking her what she read she replied, *The Bombay Guardian* and *The Times of India*. It is pleasant to see how much attached they become to those who visit them, bringing some life and brightness from the world outside.

"One Hindoo, of good caste, comes to me for Christian instruction. She is a nice young wife, and her prejudices against our religion are lessening. She sat down to tea with us one day, and that was a great step in advance. She learns the Elementary Catechism well, and reads Barth's 'Bible History' with understanding. The difficulty with Hindoos is, that their religion is so interwoven with every detail of their social life, that the embracing of Christianity is not only a change of creed, but a revolution in almost every particular."

CHAPTER VI.

WORK AMONG THE VILLAGES.

DR. McGEORGE and Miss Moore, a companion missionary, had for some time cherished a desire to visit a few of the scattered villages lying outside the bounds of their regular daily work, and in pursuance of this determination they set forth in the early part of the year 1888—Miss Moore taking charge of the evangelistic, and Miss McGeorge the medical department. As the following letter will prove, they had a most encouraging tour, carrying spiritual light and physical healing wherever they went, and winning the affection and goodwill of the native women. The accommodation was sometimes rather modest; but such considerations had no weight with the devoted mission workers. The first letter we have relating to this tour is dated from Khadama, one of the villages a few miles south of Ahmedabad. It speaks of the abundance of monkeys, parrots, and gay-coloured flowers; but adds. "You will shortly have primroses. How lovely primroses are! So fresh and sweet! No fragrant flowers bloom here; we have colour in abundance, but little fragrance. No sweet songsters of the grove, but gay parrots. The parrots fly about the streets in Ahmedabad."

As the ladies had no tent with them, they had to accept any accommodation available. We find them in this journey lodged in the local church buildings, presumably belonging to the Mission. Miss McGeorge says: "Miss Moore and I arranged some months ago to visit these villages in the cold season, and that I should bring medicines. Accordingly, we came. We are living in the church: a plain building, more like a barn than a church, except that it has a verandah at two sides. We have a table and chairs, and that is about all. The vestry is our sleeping-room. The church is near the village of Khadama, where, and in some other villages, there are Christians. On Sunday we have two services, conducted by a native agent, who does wonderfully well. You would be surprised, and perhaps taken aback, at the appearance of the flock in church. To begin with, there are no seats whatever; they all sit on the floor, gathered up in a heap, and in Christian fashion, take off their turbans. Now, considering that in Oriental fashion they also doff their shoes, you can imagine they present a rather wild appearance—bare legs, feet, and head; hair unkempt, black, and often long, except in some cases where they conform to the heathen practice of shaving the head, leaving only a top-knot for the god to lift them up to heaven with when they die! Some of them stand at singing—some remain inert. The singing itself is something very terrible to listen to—three or four different keys all striving for the mastery, the ambition being who should shout the loudest.

"To reach the heathen, we go to a village every morning, accompanied by a Bible-woman, who works under a Bible-woman at Borsad all the year round. We gather the women around us, and they having provided Miss Moore and me with a native bed to sit on, the Bible-woman first sings a hymn, and then talks about the subject of it a little. Afterwards Miss Moore addresses them, and they listen attentively, and seem to comprehend. During the day patients come to me; I have had 424 so far. . . . Last week we went to Pandoli, . . . A little brick-building had been arranged as a dispensary. It was carpeted, and had flowers on the table. The gate was closed to all but women, and a Sepoy kept order, for outside there was a great crowd of men. We hope soon to have visited the whole seventeen villages."

Another letter tells of the first administration of the Lord's Supper in Borsad, and the feelings with which Dr. Mary McGeorge regarded the, to her, sacred spot.

"It was very interesting to visit Borsad, the first station of our Mission, and to see the spot, on the roof of a gateway, where the Lord's Supper was first dispensed in Gujerat. . . . The drive back to Anand was very amusing; the bullocks could scarcely be prevailed upon to go at all, and some of them at length lay down in a pond. It is a matter of great thankfulness that our Heavenly Father has granted me health and strength; but then, seeing He brought me here, He will faithfully protect me from all harm. . . . I never have time for fancy work now, and am in danger of forgetting all such feminine accomplishments."

Sometimes she records friendly ministrations on the part of the women. Thus, at Khadama—

"The women seem to understand our motive in coming so far. Yesterday we went to Jogan, a village of about 900 inhabitants. After we had finished talking with them, one friendly woman asked, 'Why could we not come and live with them?' She said they would give us of their food, and consider it greater merit than to feed the Brahmins. They said they had heard of Jesus two years ago from Miss Moore; but how could we expect them to know anything when visited only once in two years. If we would come every week they might know something, etc., etc. At the dispensary, which we erected *pro tem.*, some men pleaded so hard to be attended to that I had to make an exception to the general rule of treating only women and children. . . . They all understand that our wish is to do them good, and one woman said that she had heard that 'we are merciful people, and would cure their diseases.' There is a great deal of neglected disease and suffering in these remote districts. . . . We are twelve miles from the nearest railway station, and the free, open life is a pleasant change from the denseness of the city."

The following account of work among the women is interesting:—"A few mornings ago I brought my Testament, and read to the waiting crowd about the Woman of Samaria. At first they did not seem to understand very well; but I went over it a second time, trying to explain a little, and then one woman in front, with a bright, intelligent face, seemed to grasp the meaning of the story, and as I read each verse, she turned to those around her and, with many gesticulations, explained it all: how the woman thought 'This is just a tired-looking man—how could she know He was the Son of God?' and how, when He said He would give her water, she wondered where He would get it from, the well being deep—and so on. The whole scene—the well—the tired traveller—the waterpots left behind while the woman hastened to the city along the hot, dusty road, and the eager crowd coming out to see all—would be vividly real to them. I wondered as I looked at the earnest, interested faces of the women if they also would believe and thirst no more."

One woman told Miss McGeorge "how weary she was of life," and for reply to her had quoted Christ's invitation to weary, heavy-laden souls. "I saw she was listening to me, so I went on to speak about the Saviour of the world. She told me she had so much misery in her life that her sole pleasure had been in the worship of God, and also told me of all her fastings and washings, and the portions of Scripture she had repeated every day."

Evidently here was an earnest seeker of the kingdom of God.

CHAPTER VII.

HOME.

THE time drew nigh for Miss McGeorge's visit home. Climate and continuous hard work had told upon her, so that her physical need of rest and change cried out for indulgence. She had given the first morning dew of her youth to the sacred work of imitating the Master; and still thought her work one of the most blessed to be found upon earth. It will not be out of place here to quote some written words of her own dealing with the opportunities and results of medical work, and reviewing the progress made.

"All doors open to a doctor, for sickness comes alike to all. 'Why do you take all this trouble?' is often asked; and when we tell them it is God who has had pity on them, and has put it into the hearts of people at home to send us out to them whom we regard as sisters they are pleased and not a little astonished. After having been in a house in a time of illness, one is ever afterwards a welcome visitor. All stiffness is laid aside and the women talk quite freely. 'Do not be afraid! she is like a mother,' is the assurance given to a timid comer who fain would join the circle, but fears the strangers. Occasionally they ask one to go even when they themselves feel convinced that the end is close at hand. 'Never mind, only come and see!' This is a very welcome invitation, because the general rule is that where hope is excluded no effort is made. In such rare cases it has once or twice been possible to turn the scale in the sick one's favour. For instance, in a fever patient who is being allowed to die merely from starvation owing to ignorance, a timely giving of suitable nourishment has carried her over the critical period, and then this unexpected result is proclaimed as a miracle. . . . It was only after three years of work among caste and outcast women that Mussulman women at last invited us into their homes, and this we attribute, under God, to the labours of a Zenana missionary who devoted as much as possible of her time to the neglected Mussulmans. It seemed as if the work among Mohammedans was just opening up attractive vistas of usefulness when an interruption on account of health shut out the prospect, for a time at least. The very last week a Mohammedan rajah brought his Ranee down from a distant state, while other places were asking for visits. Only those who understand the pain of having to refuse much-needed help can enter into the feelings of such as have to leave the happy work in this city, knowing that there is no one left behind to carry it on."

Dr. Mary McGeorge left Ahmedabad in November, 1890, for home, on a year's furlough—this furlough, however, being afterwards extended to two years. Reaching Bombay, she embarked on board the P. and O. steamer sailing for London. Disembarking at Southampton, a few days were spent with her sisters in Bath, and with friends in London and elsewhere. The weather at this season was very severe, the snow lying deep, more especially in the South of England. The change, within a few days, from the genial warmth of the Mediterranean to the biting wintry winds was felt intensely, and she suffered keenly for a time. On her journey from Ahmedabad to Bombay she had been attacked, while at Surat, by malarial fever, but hastened forward and had the good fortune to find the feverish symptoms disappear the moment she reached the sea-board. They gave her no trouble whilst at sea, but when the journey was fairly over, and she had settled down in the house of her brother—E. G. McGeorge, Esq., J.P., at Belfast—the fever returned, and ran its normal course—the ague for some days being very troublesome.

To all appearance her constitution was very seriously shaken, but she rapidly gained strength, and though for some considerable time unable to undertake any public work, was preparing herself for further usefulness during her holiday. She felt that her life was wholly devoted to her special branch of service, so that her one wish in India or at home was to forward the interests of Zenana missions.

In pursuance of this desire she addressed many missionary assemblies in furtherance of Zenana and medical work. It was recognised by all how fully her heart was in her vocation; and wherever she spoke fresh interest was awakened. The work received a great impetus, and the assemblies she addressed were spellbound.

In the early part of 1891, while Miss McGeorge's own health was but feeble, she was called to the bedside of a brother who was lying ill, almost on the verge of the grave. Loving devotion and constant attention, however, turned the scale, so that in about three weeks the patient was out of danger.

For the last three months of her visit home Miss McGeorge was with her sisters in Bath. On looking back to these happy days of her stay with them, her friends could afterwards recall how frequently she spoke of the possibility of never again returning home, so much had she suffered from the climate during her first term of service. At such times she would say, "I do not expect to return. I will die at my post." At other times she took a more hopeful view, and discussed plans for her final retirement; but not until she had given the best of her life to her work. She looked upon the Zenana Medical Mission as her own life's mission, and resisted all overtures to turn her talents to account in the civil sphere.

It was noticeable during the last few months that her spiritual experiences were remarkable, as if to fit her for the closing scene of life. It can now be recognised by those who knew her, that her spirit seemed to be fast ripening for heaven; she was the possessor of that perfect peace which "passeth all understanding." Every possible moment was spent in close, earnest, loving study of the Bible, in order also to be able to impart instruction to her Indian sisters.

During her furlough, and, in consequence of frequent conferences with the Zenana Committee, she had arranged for several new departures in connection with her work in India. A large tent was ordered for her use for journeys outside the cities, through villages. Such a structure was felt to be absolutely necessary—by night as a place of rest, and by day as a place of shelter and residence: a dispensary and a waiting-room combined. Lady missionaries, when out among the villages, are often put to much inconvenience in consequence of unsuitable accommodation; and it was supposed that the tent would remedy that, beside adding to the comfort and efficiency of the workers. She had also set her heart on having a hospital in Ahmedabad, seeing the absolute need of such an adjunct to all medical work in India.

The sojourn at Bath drew to an end, and the natural sorrow at the immediate severance from her much-loved sisters cast its shadow over her. But she maintained her brave spirit. In one of her last letters she writes: "I must say 'good-bye'—yes, for ever, on this side of the river. Mrs. Beatty" (the wife of another missionary), "and I are going in the steamer *Roumania*, of the Anchor Line." Mrs. Beatty had been at home in England for some years on account of delicate health, and Miss McGeorge had arranged with Mrs. Beatty that they would return together. She left Bath on the 21st of October, 1892, and was accompanied as far as Birkenhead by one of her sisters. Her last letter home was dated Birkenhead, the 22nd of October, 1892, and in it she says: "We have been down to the *Roumania*. It is small, but comfortable. We go on board finally at five o'clock this evening. All has gone nicely so far, and will, I am sure, continue to do so. Things promise well. Good-bye. Don't forget me." During the night of the 22nd of October the *Roumania* steamed away on her last voyage, a full week behind her appointed date. Humanly speaking, that week's delay was her destruction. But we cannot tell, after all. We must look away from second causes to the great First Cause and Disposer of all things, even of life and death. There are no "happenings" with God; "The Lord reigneth," and this fact proves the only consolation of believing souls in times of darkness and sorrow.

The weather was known to be stormy and foggy, but no one seemed to have apprehended danger. The continual safety of missionary passengers in their numerous voyages to and fro had passed into a proverb, so that seafaring men have been heard to express the wish to have a missionary on board. But now two missionaries were to ascend to the "Father's House" through the medium of a "chariot of waters."

On the morning of Saturday, the 29th of October, the news began to be whispered in England that the *Roumania* was lost off the coast of Portugal. Only a few persons were aware, however, of the importance of the *Roumania's* safety to the Irish Presbyterian Church. As the day wore on fuller information came to hand, and, ere evening closed, it was known that the vessel had gone down, and that only nine souls were saved, while among the "lost" were the two lady missionaries. As this became realised, the feeling of the Irish Presbyterians was intense; in fact, no circumstance had so moved this branch of Christ's Church for over fifty years. In one short hour, the wife of one faithful missionary, going out to rejoin her husband, and the devoted lady Zenana doctor, going forth to resume her work, were cut off amidst a howling, angry tempest and a raging sea, whose cold, cruel waters knew neither pity nor tenderness. As we said before, only nine souls were saved; the others all rest, either in their ocean-bed, or in the little sea-side graveyard, until the resurrection morn. Then, among those who come forth to meet the Master, for whom they sacrificed, laboured, and lost their lives, will be Dr. Mary McGeorge and her friend.

The investigations of the Rev. Mr. Jeffrey, a gentleman sent out by the Irish Presbyterian Mission Board, seemed to establish the fact that Mrs. Beatty's body had been washed ashore, and interred with others in the churchyard of Serros Bouros, on the Portuguese coast. But the most vigilant search could not discover the body of Dr. Mary McGeorge. Down in her ocean-grave, among seaweeds and rocks, rest her remains until that day, when "the sea shall give up her dead." But Mary McGeorge has the limitless ocean for a tomb, and the truth of God, which she taught to the ignorant, idolatrous women of India, shall doubtless bear blessed fruit in that land "where there is no more sea." Until the resurrection trump shall sound, her remains rest, although uncoffined and unknown, in the safe, sure keeping of our Father. And in that confidence, faith must rest and be quiet.

> "So she took
> The one grand step beyond the stars of God,
> Into the splendour, shadowless and broad,
> Into the everlasting joy and light,
> The zenith of her earthly life was come!

> "What then? Eye hath not seen, ear hath not heard,
> Wait till thou, too, hast fought the noble strife,
> And won, through Jesus Christ, the Crown of Life!
> *Then*, thou shalt know the glory of the Word;
> *Then*, as the stars for ever, ever shine,
> Beneath the King's own smile, perpetual zenith thine."

RIVER BOATS.

MARY LOUISA WHATELY.

Mary Louisa Whately:

THE STORY OF HER MISSION LIFE AND WORK IN EGYPT.

CHAPTER I.

THE PREPARATION.

> "Jesus! Master! take me, use me!
> I belong to Thee;
> Thou art mine! my life shall serve Thee,
> Through eternity."

MARY LOUISA WHATELY was the second daughter and third child of Archbishop Whately of Dublin. She was, however, born on the 31st of August, 1824, at Halesworth, in Suffolk, of which parish her father was then rector. In 1827 Dr. Whately removed to Oxford, having been appointed to the principalship of Alban Hall. From this post he was translated to Dublin as Archbishop in 1831, and from this date Dublin continued to be the much-loved home of Mary Whately. She is described by her sister as being a quick, intelligent child, with a retentive memory;

very ardent and impulsive, hot-tempered and generous, possessing a great faculty for picking up knowledge of all kinds, and capability for turning her knowledge to account. The conversation and reading carried on in the Whately home conduced very much to the mental development of Mary and her sisters.

Outside the family the children were encouraged to be useful. The mother wisely trained them to remember the poor and needy, as well as to teach the children in the schools of Dublin, and to distribute kindly gifts to the poor in a judicious and systematic way. And so wisely did Mrs. Whately train her daughters how to give, that for months, at one time, they had been saving their pocket-money in order to purchase some of the loaves and meat destined to be distributed; thus learning to exemplify true lives of unselfish devotion. Mrs. Whately often employed Mary and her sisters in doing missions of mercy and kindness among the residents of Stillorgan. Archbishop Whately had opened a National School in his grounds for the benefit of the village children, and in this school the sisters were delighted to teach classes. Further, they employed their ready pens in the production of reading-books for use in the Irish National Schools. Mary Whately was thus in these various ways being trained for the work of her later life in Egypt.

During the days of the terrible Irish famine,—between the years 1846 and 1851,—the Whatelys were much engaged in Irish Church Mission work, as carried on by Protestants among the Irish Roman Catholics. Mary received an undoubted spiritual blessing in carrying out this mission to the poor and starving, for, according to her sister, she "always declared that at this period the turning-point in her religious life came." And, naturally, with the deepening of her spiritual life, came the increased desire for active work for God. Accordingly she, with her sisters, laboured "more abundantly" in Ragged Schools and Irish Church Mission Homes, doing good as opportunity offered to waifs and strays of humanity. It is suggestive that the worker among "Ragged Life in Egypt" did not in these early days disdain ragged life in Ireland.

Hospital work at this time also claimed Miss Whately and her sister. There happened to be in the providence of God, about the end of the Crimean War, a considerable influx of destitute Italians into Dublin. Mary Whately and her sisters visited these poor foreigners at their homes, and the sick ones at the hospitals. In this way she learnt the art of communicating religious instruction to those of different races and faiths. By all these ministries she became proficient in the ministry of explaining Biblical truth to those of opposing religions, customs, and superstitions,—a gift which stood her in good stead in the coming years of her cherished life-work.

At length an opportunity for foreign mission-work presented itself. In the winter of 1856 she was recommended to visit Cairo for the sake of her health, and did so, accompanied by a friend. The following somewhat lengthy extract, written near the end of her life, accurately describes her feelings at her entrance into this "open door" of service. She says :—

"More than thirty years have passed since I first looked on the shining shores of Egypt. A calm, blue sea, with glittering light on its faint ripples, a distant view of white minaret towers, and feathery palms just visible on the flat line of coast, a crowd of shipping in the harbour before us, with many coloured flags waving gently in the faint morning breezes, and strange groups of men, black, white, and brown, in little boats, rowing hither and thither, and chattering in unknown tongues,—over all, the indescribable atmosphere of the sunny south, bright and clear, throwing deep purple shadows in strong contrast with the intense light. I see it all now in memory's eye as plainly as if the scene were actually present; and I recollect the bewildered sensation of stepping on shore, dizzy with the long rough sea passage in a wretched old steamer, and of forgetting fatigue and everything else at the sight of a string of camels. 'Look at them!' I said to my companion; 'we are really in Africa.'

"Who that has studied Scripture does not feel a thrill of delight as he looks for the first time on these creatures—at once awkward and graceful, with their spongy feet lifted and set down with solemn cautiousness—their long necks turned occasionally from side to side, the large beautiful dark eyes glancing round with an expression of dignified contempt? How many times we have read of Abraham and his servant, and of Rebekah alighting from her camel, and of Job with his three thousand camels?

"Then we made our way towards the hotel, slowly and on foot, for in those days there were scarcely any carriages in Alexandria, and we preferred walking after the cart on which baggage had been placed, to riding on donkeys, as the native saddles were strange. Very different is everything now in the same city, which has become more than half European. It is only the sunshine that is quite unchanged. As we moved along the unpaved street, from the harbour to the hotel, the groups were all so curious and interesting, that I kept pausing every moment to observe

CITY OF CAIRO.

them. Here a Bedouin from the desert in goat's hair mantle, or flowing white woollen robes, and red and yellow striped *Kuffieh* on his head, his red leather

BEDOUIN WOMEN AND CHILDREN.

girdle supporting a knife in a sheath, and an old-fashioned gun on his shoulder, was standing with a comrade at a little rude stall where huge water-melons displayed their dark green rinds and bright crimson pulp, as the thirsty wayfarers devoured the juicy slices, glancing around meantime with what I afterwards learnt to know as the genuine Bedouin look—which seems 'nought to mark, but all to spy.'

"A little further on were a party of native women in their dark blue garments, limp and soft, falling in graceful (if dirty) folds, as they sat on the dusty ground or stood leaning against a bit of ruined wall, some wearing the face veil of black crape tied under the eyes, which I then saw for the first time; others being of the poorest class, with face uncovered. Little brown children, half naked and miserably neglected in appearance, clung to their shoulders or squatted beside them in the dust. Next, a party of wealthy merchants would pass with their long robes of rich cloth and beautiful striped native silk, setting off their dusky complexion. Numbers of men and boys of the humbler class were mixed with them, hurrying to or from the harbour on some errand, their arms and legs bare, and their only garments white or blue cotton shirts, but all, rich or poor, had turbans. The red tarboosh, now common among many of the poor, and most of the higher class, was then a mark of Turks or Europeans, or Syrians; now worn by most gentlemen, it was then confined to Levantines, or visitors. Every group was a picture then, and the prevalence of rich colours in so clear an atmosphere, was enough to delight the eye of anyone who had a love of the picturesque. But it was most strange and confusing to hear all around a language so entirely different in sound from any of the European tongues with which I was more or less familiar. Altogether I felt like a person in a dream.

"Two days afterwards we were on our way to

Cairo. The primitive oriental life had already been changed by the introduction of the first European railroad, which had been completed about a year before. It was October, and most of the Delta was under water, the inundation having been heavy that year, and that part of Egypt being entirely flat and with very few trees. Here, all there was to see were little groups of mud huts with bundles of reeds by way of roof, and a large sycamore fig-tree or a few palms near them standing like islands on slightly raised plots of ground, with water all around, and buffaloes standing half submerged evidently enjoying their bath extremely. Whenever we stopped at a station, a troop of excessively dirty children clamoured for 'backsheesh,' and frightful old women with faces like walnut shells, bleared eyes and dangling rags, offered baskets of sticky dates covered with leaves, which feebly protected them from the swarms of flies.

"Young girls passed up and down the platforms at every station with the porous water-vessels of the country, offering drink to travellers with the cry, 'Cold water, O ye thirsty!' in a sweet half-plaintive tone. Every one was hot and thirsty, for early in October, in Egypt, the weather is still like summer (a good deal hotter than some English summers, indeed), and many hands were stretched out for the vessel of water, and gladly were the coppers demanded paid; but as we passed on and the little water-sellers were left far behind, my heart ached for them and for all the rest in their land, because they had never heard the blessed invitation, 'Ho! every one that thirsteth, come ye to the waters,' and knew nothing of the water of life which Jesus Christ, our Lord, gives to them that ask, 'without money, and without price.'"

This sketch graphically describes Miss Whately's

first impressions of the land which was to be her home for so many long years. Still, however, one obstacle and another kept her from entering upon her life-work. After spending this winter of 1856 in Cairo, she joined a party of friends going to the Holy Land in 1857, and revelled in the beauty of the Anti-Lebanon, ending with a visit to Damascus—the oldest city in the world. The party of travellers spent a month on the Mount of Olives and its environs, and she became so interested in the work being carried on among the young Jewesses of Jerusalem, that after her return home, in the summer of 1857, it was a scheme very much laid upon her heart to revisit Jerusalem, and engage in mission work there. But God, who "has His plan for every man," had His plan for Mary Whately.

In 1860, bereavement visited the home of the Whatelys, and both the mother and youngest sister died within the space of a few weeks. A long winter of anxious care and nursing, followed by deep sorrow, had its effect in undermining Mary's health so seriously that it was feared by the medical man that her lungs were affected. He advised her spending the following winter in a southern climate, and Mary's thoughts immediately turned to the Egyptian city where she had formerly visited, and gained her first Eastern experiences. During that preliminary visit she had become acquainted with Mrs. Leider, wife of a Church Missionary living there, and so had made some acquaintance with mission work. Thither, therefore, she resolved to go, believing that Providence had opened a way for her to make educational and Christian efforts on behalf of the Moslem women and girls—a hitherto much-neglected class of the population of Egypt.

CHAPTER II.

BEGINNING WORK.

> "He that winneth souls is wise,
> In the gracious Master's eyes,
> Well may we contented be,
> To be counted fools for Thee.
> So may we redeem the time,
> That with every evening chime,
> Our rejoicing hearts may see
> Blood-bought souls brought back to Thee.'
>
> F. R. HAVERGAL.

THE winter of 1860 found Miss Whately in Cairo, with a cousin. After spending a few weeks with Mrs. Leider, she took a house in Cairo, in this way accomplishing two objects—making a temporary home for herself and friend, and gaining an opportunity of doing good to the female population of Cairo. It was doubtless the first effort made on behalf of Moslem females since the rise of the False Prophet, some 1200 years before, and, as such, is full of interest. The reader will best appreciate the story if given in her own words. She says:—

"At the period of my first visit to Egypt, I saw little but the outside of things, but when circumstances brought me there a second time, it was laid on my heart to try and do something for the girls and women of the land, especially those of the Moslem poorer classes—by far the most numerous, of course. The only schools hitherto opened for the children of the land had no scholars except from the Copts or native Christians; others were considered quite out of reach, and many of my friends endeavoured to dissuade me from an attempt, which, they said, was sure to end in failure. However, it seemed best to make an effort at all events. I was aware, indeed, of the great bigotry of the people, and of their utter indifference to female education. Even a short residence and very little acquaintance with the language were sufficient to convince me of these facts, and to show that the work must be slow, for it was all up-hill. But it was begun in prayer, and, therefore, difficulties and delays did not greatly discourage me.

"First, a place of residence had to be found, not nearly so easy a matter as in these days. There were comparatively few new houses, and the old ones were apt to be extremely dirty, and the wood-work full of vermin. A new one was recommended by a gentleman who assisted my cousin and myself in our search. It was not quite finished, but after visiting some of the old ones, we thought it had the fewer disadvantages on the whole. It stood at the corner of a street not quite so narrow as many others, where the inhabitants of the opposite dwellings could not shake hands across, as would be possible in some cases. It looked out on a lane on the other side, and this lane was occupied by curiously tumbledown abodes, with a few mud huts here and there between the more pretentious buildings, partly stone, and partly mud brick. This neighbourhood was desirable, however, as enabling the poor people to be visited easily. A coffee-house of a humbler sort was exactly under the window of the chief room in this house, and several small shops on the opposite side of the street, with some apartments above them, were occupied by wealthy people apparently.

"The house was so new itself that the staircase

was incomplete as yet. The walls were not plastered nor the windows glazed, nor the doors put up, and to crown all, the workmen were actually lying on the floor upon heaps of shavings, fast asleep, though it was ten o'clock in the morning! It appeared afterwards that in order to prevent them from leaving their work, they had been locked into the house, and thus afforded a fine example of forced labour.

"As it was not to be painted till a year had elapsed, the work really need not have taken more than a few days. The owner promised 'on his head' that in seven days all should be perfectly ready; but when, on the eighth day, his future tenants (who had, according to custom, paid in advance), presented themselves at the door, humbly following on foot an ox-cart containing their effects, he looked as much amazed as if they had done something unexpected indeed in believing his word! Yet it was the only chance for the tenants to get all things finished, to be on the spot, inhabiting such rooms as were habitable, otherwise the year might have rolled on to its close, and the house remained just as it was.

"The outside was clean and white; but it certainly required some courage to enter the scene of litter and confusion within. We had to spring over pools of whitewash, and clamber over loose stones, in order to reach the stairs, where we were met by a troop of dirty, half-clad boys and girls, with hods of mortar on their heads, and pails of water in their hands. Threading our way through this ragged regiment, we reached the first storey, and found at last doors and windows; but the former, having no locks or latches, obstinately refused to remain shut, till the maid who accompanied me, an energetic little Irishwoman, gave it a *slam*, and then it shut and would not open, and we remained prisoners for some time, till our new cook, a Syrian of stalwart proportions, heard our cry of distress from below, and came and forced the door open with his shoulders."

After more adventures of the kind described, Miss Whately and her helper finally settled in the still unfinished house, determined to try what could be done in the way of educational experiments for the much-neglected Egyptian maidens. And, seeing that the custom of early marriages forced the girls to leave school when about twelve years of age, there was no time to be lost. Miss Whately says on this point :—

"The wish for some sort of education for girls, though a very slight and important one, had for several years been spreading in Egypt. Among the wealthy a teacher who can instruct the young ladies in the harem in French, and perhaps a little piano, as European music is called, is frequent, though not universal; and among the middle classes in the great towns many parents are willing, if any pains are taken about it, to allow these girls to attend schools under European superintendence, and even to pay a trifle towards their teaching. Though thousands are plunged in utter ignorance in the towns, and in *all* the villages, still the schoolmistress is abroad. But when I came to Egypt in 1860, there was not a Mohammedan girls' school in Cairo, or any other Egyptian town. Everyone of whom I inquired assured me that the masses of the humbler class, being both indifferent to education in itself, and disposed to look with aversion on Christians, would never consent to let me have their little daughters in a school; while the right sort of girls were shut up, and therefore quite out of reach. 'One can never say that anything is a failure which has never been tried,' was my answer. They smiled and shrugged their shoulders, and left me to my obstinacy.

"The only teacher to be found after many inquiries was a worthy Christian matron, who could read in the only book she was accustomed to, which was the New Testament, and the narrative parts of the books of Genesis and Exodus. She had a young daughter of thirteen, who had been to school at Beyrout, and could read as well as write fairly. But to secure the services of the good woman and her girl, we had to accommodate the whole family, as there was no cheap lodging near at hand, and though inconvenient, we had space enough, including the use of the schoolroom after school. Behold the teacher, therefore, with her five children (her husband was out on business till the evening), seated in the new room, swept and prepared with clean mats, and a few books, but no scholars. The servant had been sent to speak to his acquaintances, but without result.

"At last the matron and I sallied forth together; my cousin was indisposed, and still confined to her room. We went rather timidly up the narrow and dirty lane on one side of our house: the other looked on a busy thoroughfare in which we should have been jostled; and besides, it was all shops, and we were seeking to speak with women who were very rarely seen in shops. The occupants of the tumble-down houses and mud huts in the lane were all at their doors, staring at the strangers. They live chiefly outside; indeed the little dark dens being used merely to sleep in. With the matron's help (she knew a little English), and my own broken Arabic, I managed to make one or two understand our errand, something in this way. 'Good morning; peace be to you.' 'Oh! peace to you, lady!' 'I see you have a nice girl there; will you let her come to our school, and learn to read, and also to sew?' The woman, who is squatted on the threshold of her hut, muffled in filthy garments, for the day is rather cold, shrugs her shoulders, and the matron interposes, and repeats what I had said, with some additions and many friendly smiles. 'We are Moslems, and our girls don't learn.' 'Oh, but it is so nice to read, sister, and she shall learn to sew, too; the lady has brought little thimbles.' (Girl, in a loud aside, 'I want a thimble.' Matron pats her on the back.) 'Yes, yes, my dear, a new thimble and needles thou shalt have.' The mother demurs. 'We don't like strangers, and girls need not learn, except to make bread or so. Why does this lady want our girls?' The matron says, 'Because she loves God, and therefore loves your children, and wants to teach them about God.' '*Mashalla!* well, we will see to-morrow; perhaps she can go.'

"After visiting ten or twelve houses and huts, besides speaking to some groups who stood about gossiping, some with babies on their shoulders, others eating oranges or sugar-cane, we at last returned with the promise of several scholars, feeling triumphant and thankful. Of course, most were only inclined to come and see what this new affair was, and even of these several were dissuaded by their neighbours from having anything to do with 'those Christians.' One woman appeared at nine o'clock next morning, wearing a quantity of silver and coral ornaments on her rounded brown arms and throat; though her dress of dark blue cotton seemed threadbare, and was far from clean. She led a nice-looking child, about nine years old, in the little white muslin veil and loose coloured frock worn by tolerably decent poor girls. Of a volley of words she poured out after the salutations, I could only make out that the child was timid, and afraid to stay, but to-morrow she would send her. The first fish was caught, and now was escaping the fisher's hand. The matron and I both caressed and spoke kindly to her; she smiled and said really she would return, and she *did;* but at the time I could not trust that she would do so, and felt rather cast-down. Half-an-hour passed, and then two little black-eyed, dirty-faced girls in ragged frocks trotted in, followed by their mothers, and I thought grand-mothers also, for several women came in, some old, some young, and there was a good deal of unveiling and chattering. The Egyptian citizen's wife, indeed, all but the very poorest in the towns, wears a black crape face veil, fastened by a brass or gold tube rather like an exaggerated thimble, which is sewn to a fillet passed round the head at one end, fastened between the eyes, and to the face veil at the other. After a little while we had more visitors, and at length the women departed, and nine little girls, from seven to ten years old, were left to begin school. No recruiting sergeant was ever so pleased as I, when I hastened upstairs to report to my invalid relative that we had actually nine pupils.

"After the names had been asked, and the little Fatmah, Zeynab, Hosna, etc. were duly inscribed on a paper, I asked each in turn, 'Who made you?' Some replied, Allah (God), but two or three said, 'Mohammed.' The first verse of the Bible, 'In the beginning God created the heaven and the earth,' was then repeated to them, and they were taught to say it, first each one by herself, and then all together. This was the *beginnings* of instruction for them, poor children. The young teacher was too inexperienced to be able to explain it, so I did what I could in that way, and then we both set to teaching the first five letters of their difficult alphabet, till they seemed to be getting tired; they were then allowed a rest, and afterwards a singing lesson was commenced. The neighbours might have supposed a set of cats to be the pupils, if they listened to the discordant sounds which the first attempt at a gamut produced. Three months later, a stranger visiting the school was delighted at the sweet singing of the hymns! The mewing and squeaking were nearly forgotten by that time.

"The children were delighted when the work-hour arrived, the real inducement to most of them and their mothers having been the needle-work. Perhaps the teachers were not sorry when every little brown finger was supplied with a new thimble, and they could sit down for a few minutes. No one who has not tried it can conceive the difficulty of teaching those who have not only no wish to learn, but no idea of what learning is, or what possible good is to be gained by all this trouble; and, of course, the strain upon the mind is greatly increased when one's knowledge of the language is very limited indeed. The children all took willingly to sewing; indeed, they had many times in the course of the forenoon thrown down the cards, and cried out, 'The work! give us the work!' The English needles and scissors gave them much pleasure, and were eagerly examined by some mothers and elder sisters who paid visits to the school-room in the course of the day to see what the foreigner was doing with their little ones, for, if ignorant, they are usually very fond parents. Some brought bread, bunches of raw carrots, or some such dainty, and after giving it to the children, would squat down on the floor to watch the proceedings.

Of course, it did rather interfere with business, but it will not do to strain a new rope too tightly, and, besides, Eastern manners are unlike ours, and I thought it wisest never to meddle with them unless some real evil was in question. On the second day we had fourteen scholars. As they entered, each kicked off her slippers, if she possessed any, at the door—I think more than half possessed some kind of shoe—and then went up to kiss the hand of the superintendent, and lay it on her head, both which processes became pleasanter when cleanly habits came more into fashion."

But Miss Whately was called home to Dublin, in the spring of 1861, and she left after placing the school, thus newly formed, under the charge of a teacher provided by the Society for Promoting Female Education in the East.

The end of 1861 and the early months of 1862 were spent at Pau with some friends, for Miss Whately felt the need of rest after her labours in Egypt. While in Pau, she, however, found work of another sort to do. A young man, the son of a Scotch minister, was sojourning there for the benefit of his health, in the care of two sisters and a brother. Miss Whately became intimate with them, and in time grew friendly enough to converse with the consumptive invalid upon eternal things. She could venture to point him to Jesus, and sang many hymns by his bedside to cheer him in his failing hours. She was a great comfort to the distressed family, after all was over, and cheered the bereaved ones in far-away Scotland, by her kind, sympathetic letters. After leaving Pau she made a little excursion, with friends, into the north of Spain, and so recruited her health for coming years of evangelistic labours in Egypt. She needed all the strength she could gain.

CHAPTER III.

SOWING BESIDE ALL WATERS.

"In the highways and hedges, go seek for the lost,
Gather them into the fold;
Was the earnest command that our Saviour Divine,
Taught His disciples of old."

DURING the winter of 1862, Miss Whately, accompanied by her faithful Irish maid, sought her mission sphere in Cairo again. But while absent the little mission school had been closed, for the teacher's health failed, and she had to remove to another sphere of labour in the East. As soon, however, as Miss Whately was again settled in her old house, she re-opened the school. The news that the school was again open soon spread, and former pupils were only too delighted to return. However, the re-opening of the school proved no slight matter, as will be seen from Miss Whately's own account of it:—

"Though but a few months had elapsed during which the little ragged school in Bab-el-Bahar had been closed, the desolate appearance of the room made it look as if it had been deserted for a much longer period. It had been no one's business to look after it particularly, and the poor little schoolroom was bare and dirty when I came to take possession of it again in the month of November, 1862. No texts or pictures as of old hung against the walls; nothing but dust, and a few torn books remained. However, it is better to look forward than to look back, and having caught a little well-known child at the door, and despatched her to look for the former scholars, and tell them, 'School was open,' I went upstairs to get some books and pictures which were stored away there, and then began to sweep the dusty room while awaiting the return of the maid, who was gone to fetch work materials, and the arrival of the new matron, who, like all Egyptians, was behind time. She was merely engaged to help in keeping order, cleaning the schoolroom, and instructing the scholars in plain sewing, and was by no means to be a teacher, being quite uneducated. No native teacher or assistant could be obtained, though I was in treaty for one, so that I was quite alone. The prospect did not look very brilliant; but help comes usually in one way or another in time of need.

"The first helper was a poor washerwoman, who, finding her former employer alone in the house expressed much surprise and pleasure in the meeting, and taking the broom almost by force from my hands, exclaimed, 'Sit down, lady, and I will sweep the room for you.' She had scarcely finished when little voices were heard on the stairs, and there was a rush of scholars, chiefly old ones, but accompanied by a few others (their younger sisters) all tumultuous in their greetings. Twenty pairs of little henna-dyed hands were eagerly held out, with deafening shouts of 'Welcome! welcome! teacher! Our teacher has come back! God be praised!' After some time had been occupied in salutations and inquiries, and recognitions, the affectionate but somewhat unruly creatures were arranged in a row on a mat, while I said a few words to them, explaining that as yet there was no teacher except myself (for the only matron I could procure did not know her letters), and that I could only read Arabic very slowly and imperfectly, but that I would do my best and would study every evening so as to know more; and on their part they must be good and obedient, and learn very nicely, which, of course, was promised readily enough.

"After a short prayer and a portion of the Gospel read and explained, they were set down to their alphabet and spelling-cards; for though some had been formerly several months at school they had forgotten in the interval, or else had made but little progress, so that none could read except two, and they with great difficulty, and only spelling each word as they went.

"Keeping a Ragged School is not a sinecure in any country, as everybody knows who has tried it, and of course it is more difficult when the language is imperfectly known, and where there was no aid such as in a long-established school can always be obtained from a monitress or teacher of some sort. The first day or two it seemed impossible to keep the little voices quiet, even for a moment. There were no habits of order or obedience, and each seemed to wish to do what was good in her own eyes. . . .

"In the course of about six weeks I was obliged to change the matron for another, who, though equally uneducated, was not so much addicted to forsaking her daily duty in the workroom, and who did not waste so much time over long cherrystick pipes. I cannot say she never smoked when she should have been cutting out needlework, or never made a pretext of going to church when a visit to her sister's to gossip and eat nuts and almonds was the second and longest part of the ceremony; but still she did much better than her predecessor in many respects. I arranged afterwards with a native embroideress to come daily and instruct part of the scholars in this popular, because lucrative, employment. They made a pretty picture, in spite of the rags of so many, when seated in little groups over the embroidery frames, the Coptic girl who taught them leaning over each set in turn, her net veil twisted gracefully across her shoulders, and a heap of bright-coloured skeins of silk lying beside her, and all the circle looking so cheerful and contented. Nor was the sight less pleasing from the contrast of what had been the daily life of these poor children before they were gathered within the walls of their school."

From the foregoing extracts our readers will without difficulty enter into the obstacles to Miss Whately's work. For some time the only teacher she could procure was a girl of Oriental and Italian parentage, who, though possessing a little knowledge of teaching, was a Romanist, and, consequently, unfit to impart religious instruction. Miss Whately, therefore, took this part of the teaching upon herself. But it was only by hard and continuous labour she could accomplish this. Her knowledge of Arabic was still so imperfect that she had to study each evening the rudiments of the language in which she was to give a lesson next day; and even while at meals a grammar or vocabulary lay on the table beside her, which she consulted by snatches. The difficulties she met with now determined her to obtain educated help, and on seeking for such, a native missionary, named Mansoor Shakoor, was recommended to her. He was about this time engaged by the Moslem Mission Society to work among Mohammedans in the East. Mansoor Shakoor served her gratuitously for some time, only working for her in his leisure hours; but as, after some time, the funds of the Moslem Mission Society failed, Miss Whately took him regularly into her employment. Shortly afterwards, finding the work growing upon her hands, she engaged the services of his brother, Joseph Shakoor.

Immediately after securing the efficient help of Mansoor Shakoor, Miss Whately started a boys' school in Cairo. But previous to the two brothers Shakoor being engaged she had made a tentative effort for the boys, stimulated thereto by the persistent beseechings of a little fellow who hung about the school daily, lamenting that he was not a girl, and could not, therefore, be admitted. Some of the boys whom she spoke to at the door of her house one day admitted that they went to Mohammedan schools, but as they spent their time in studying the Koran, and often received severe beatings, they ran away very often. Accordingly, when Miss Whately gave them the offer of attending her school on one day in the week, several lads were only too delighted to come.

The first Sunday she had to go out to look for scholars, though several had promised to come. She says: "They were a ragged and dirty crew, as may be imagined. I can scarcely say how many we had that day, as two or three went and others came; but I think nine stayed. These were clad in blue or white shirts, or rather garments which had formerly been so, but were now nearly undistinguishable, and cotton caps on their little cropped heads. Certainly dress had not done much for them; but they had bright, intelligent eyes, which lit up as they glanced curiously at the pictures on the wall. The younger ones all clamoured to stay with the lady; so I divided them from the older boys, giving these over to the young Copt who was my assistant that day."

From that day the boys' Sunday school went on and increased. The brothers Shakoor were able soon to take the general management of the school, as well as enter into other branches of her work. She was the more glad of this, as in the autumn of 1863 the death of her father, Archbishop Whately, called her home. She merely returned to Dublin to arrange needful family matters, and returned again, resolving to settle permanently in Cairo, and devote both life and fortune to her work there.

Having returned and resumed her life-work, Miss Whately found it necessary to hire another house, seeing that the two schools already in operation had so grown that her own dwelling-house could not accommodate them all. Finally, she found it necessary to erect a building; and, as 1869 brought H.R.H. the Prince of Wales on a visit to Egypt, he interceded with Ismail Pacha on her behalf for a grant of land upon which to build. The land was given; and as it lay just outside the old wall of Cairo, the Khedive made the stipulation that the buildings should be spacious and handsome, as they would be seen from the road. She set to work to obtain contributions in aid from English friends; but in the end, spent a sum of not less than three thousand pounds out of her private fortune on the undertaking. In order to do this she practised the most rigid self-denial, and refused many luxuries and much needful rest in order to attain the desired ends.

Having teachers now to conduct her mission schools, Miss Whately spent much time in visiting among the poor in the streets and lanes of Cairo, as well as in the Bedouin huts outside the town. She also treated the sick and disabled, as far as eye diseases were concerned, and wounded limbs. In spite of dirt, disorder, and neglect she did all these tasks cheerfully as unto the Lord, and was blessed by the poor and suffering as she walked about, like her

Master, on her errands of mercy. As one result, we are told, that in many places where she had formerly been pelted with dust, and called a "cursed Nazarene," she was now met by salutations of blessing and respect. "Sitt Mariam" (Lady Mary) became a household word in Cairo. So much did she see of the benefits of visiting the Egyptian women at their own homes, that she finally engaged a native convert as Bible-woman to carry on this branch of the mission work.

The elder brother Shakoor married in 1864 a young girl from the Lebanon, who afterwards became as dear to Miss Whately as an adopted child, and a valuable coadjutor in the mission work. The two brothers entered most fully into every branch of the Mission; superintending the schools, training the teachers, reading the Gospel in the native coffee-houses, and itinerating on the Nile, preaching and teaching as they went. A depot for Bibles and other books was opened in Cairo, and kept open for several years; but after it was closed, under pressure of Moslem intolerance, Miss Whately used to make a missionary journey up the Nile every spring, reading, teaching, and giving away portions of Scripture to all who could read, and who begged for them. For these excursions Miss Whately hired a dahabyeh, or native boat, making it serve as a home by day, and a sleeping-place by night. During the course of ten or twelve days she was enabled to visit many riverside villages, read, teach, distribute gospels, and attend to cases of wounds or bad eyes, so imitating her Master, who "went about doing good."

Miss Whately's mission dahabyeh was eagerly welcomed by the dwellers in the Nile villages. The first sight of the little vessel flying the English flag brought eager crowds down to the landing-places, crying: "Here are the people of the Book!" "Have you books for us?" "Come to our house and read

ON THE BANKS OF THE NILE—A DAHABYEH.

to us!" Then groups of women and children would assemble round Miss Whately and Mrs. Shakoor, who would sit down on the first available mound or fallen tree, and tell or read some of the Bible stories. Afterwards little portions of Scripture and text would be distributed to the men and boys who could read. On one of these journeys, Miss Whately supported a young girl while the English doctor performed a trying operation for the eyes, and afterwards supplied the nourishing diet required by the patient for some time. These things so impressed the old grandmother that she cried, "These ladies will be sure to go to Ferdoos!" (Paradise).

These medical ministrations were found to be so beneficial to the poor *fellaheen*, that, in 1879, a medical mission was added to the other branches of the work. The younger sister of Mrs. Shakoor was married to a skilful Syrian doctor who had been trained in the American Medical College at Beyrout, and as he was desirous of settling in Egypt, Miss Whately eagerly embraced the opportunity of engaging him for her medical mission work. A dispensary was opened near the school buildings, and several thousand patients were treated annually. Every week-day the dispensary was opened in the early morning hours to the crowds of patients, and Miss Whately delighted to be there every morning, sitting in the midst of a group of women, reading, talking, or recounting Bible stories to the waiting sufferers. After her visit to the dispensary, she made her way to the schools, over which she still kept a general supervision, assisted by Mrs. Shakoor.

We find, in her letters at this time, scattered sentences which indicate the longing for rest. One sentence runs thus:—" I long so for the end of warfare —for the Prince of Peace. Like old Doolittle, who wrote ever so long ago, I say, 'Why tarry the wheels of His chariot? Didst thou say, dear Lord, "a little while, and he that shall come will not tarry"?' To my waiting heart it seemeth a long while."

In later years, she opened a European branch school for Jewish and Syrian girls of mixed parentage; and she found it necessary to devote as much time each day as could be spared from other duties, to teach in this latest educational offshoot. She says in reference to this: "Now and then, on Saturdays or holidays, I take an early donkey ride at 6 A.M. Then, after breakfast and family reading, I go to my poor at the Dispensary, for a time varying from three-quarters of an hour to an hour and a-half, according to numbers. Then I go to my class at the Levantine School, for their Scripture lesson. At the Arab Girls' School they have now a fairly efficient teacher, and having only one tongue to teach in makes it easier. The variety of tongues and religions at the Levantine School makes me feel that I am more needed there just now, though, of course, I go in and out of the others as time will allow."

Her next journey up the Nile in her missionary dahabyeh brought to light some very encouraging incidents. In some of the riverside villages, an eager spirit of seeking for knowledge about the Christian religion was manifest, as the following extract from her journal of this date will prove: "'Bring out the aged, that they may hear the Word of God before they die!' These words were uttered by some poor Egyptian peasants, who, with a group of dark-veiled women and children were crowded round a lady seated on a native mat on the ground, near a large village a few hundred yards from the Nile. It was during the last week of the old year; a Bible was in the lady's hand, and she was reading from it, pausing to explain every now and then in a simple and intelligible manner, the hearers being mostly extremely ignorant and all Mohammedans.

"Mrs. Shakoor and myself were on our usual missionary trip, but untoward weather and a wretched boat had hindered our progress, and time was very short; still we had the happiness of finding that the good seed brought in two previous visits to this village (containing upwards of 1000 inhabitants) had not all fallen by the wayside. Several came to the boat afterwards to beg for 'the Book.' And the poor old people who were brought out to hear the Word of God read and explained, bent forward, listening as if for dear life."

She adds: "There were several in that village who seem to have caught hold of the hem of His garment. They are still weak and ignorant, and shut in by bigotry and the danger of death, from publicly avowing how far they are changed, but there is reason to think that some will be amongst the ransomed, by-and-by, when the Lord comes to take home His own."

Miss Whately was always most interested in the condition of the women of Egypt. The lot of the women belonging to the poorer classes was more tolerable than that of the richer classes, in that it was freer, and had more variety about it. Much of the woman's life was spent out of doors, assisting the husband in cultivating the little rice-patch, and similar outdoor occupations; but the women of the richer homes were kept strictly confined to the harem. It was in these latter homes that female slavery flourished, for the number of women kept in the harem was only limited by the master's means, and, frequently, slaves were added to the household. She says: "The rule is that women, not forced by the poverty of their husbands to work for daily bread by helping to cultivate the land, if in the country, or performing errands in the towns, are kept in prison—yes, prison is not too strong a word. The grand harems of the wealthy are chiefly occupied by fair Circassians and Georgians, to the number, sometimes, of many hundreds."

The year 1888 dawned, and with it the last year of Miss Whately's ministry for the women of Egypt. In the beginning of that year, she made her last visit to England, but she seemed full of life and vigour, so that her friends little dreamt that they were seeing her for the last time. In the summer she went to Switzerland with a sister and niece, and all three much enjoyed the visit. She returned to Cairo in the early autumn—Mrs. Shakoor and her family welcoming her with much rejoicing—and resumed the old employments.

In February, 1889, she chartered a dahabyeh for her usual voyage up the Nile, fearing to delay, though she was not well, for the season was advanced, and the river had fallen unusually low. She had caught a severe cold, and the keen winds that prevailed on the Nile at that time did not conduce to recovery. From her "Last Nile Notes," jotted down each evening, and preserved by her sister, we find that she resumed the old occupations of reading and talking to the villagers, many of whom remembered her, and came eagerly forth to listen to her readings and talks. After visiting the last village, she felt so ill that she returned home "to rest," and, after a day or two, consented to call in medical aid. At first it was hoped that she had only a sharp bronchial attack, and that it would soon yield to medical treatment, but ultimately congestion of the lungs came on, and the case became complicated. Friday, the 8th of

March, was a terrible day of anxiety for those who watched around her, but toward evening the worst symptoms appeared to be yielding, and both doctors reported her to be going on well when they left for the night. She had a good night, but woke in much pain in the morning. Hot applications were used, and the local pains yielded, but a sudden paleness and coldness caused Mrs. Shakoor to fear that the heart was affected. She immediately called the doctor, who confirmed her worst fears, and only a few minutes later she saw a great change come on. She bent over the sufferer and said, "You are going to Jesus, dear mamma—going to glory!" Only one bright look of response was given, and then all was over; Mary Whately's happy spirit passed away to be for ever with the Lord whom she had so lovingly served for so many years. She was called "up higher" on the 9th of March, 1889.

It may not be out of place to quote the opinion of a gentleman who has travelled much in the East, by way of conclusion. He wrote: "In my experience among Easterns of all classes and religions, and various agencies in the East, Miss Mary Louisa Whately's Mission stands first. It has reached *the very heart of Islam*, and has been the first to plant the Gospel of our Divine Master in the very midst of the Mohammedan families in Egypt. Such a thing was never heard of before, nor has been done by any one since the rise and progress of the Mohammedan religion. God has manifestly watered the seed, and blessed it also, which she scattered in faith in Egypt, and even before she was called away to the higher service, the fruits of her labours of love began to appear."

www.ingramcontent.com/pod-product-compliance
Lightning Source LLC
Chambersburg PA
CBHW030319170426
43202CB00009B/1064